THE
CROCHET
BLOCK
BIBLE

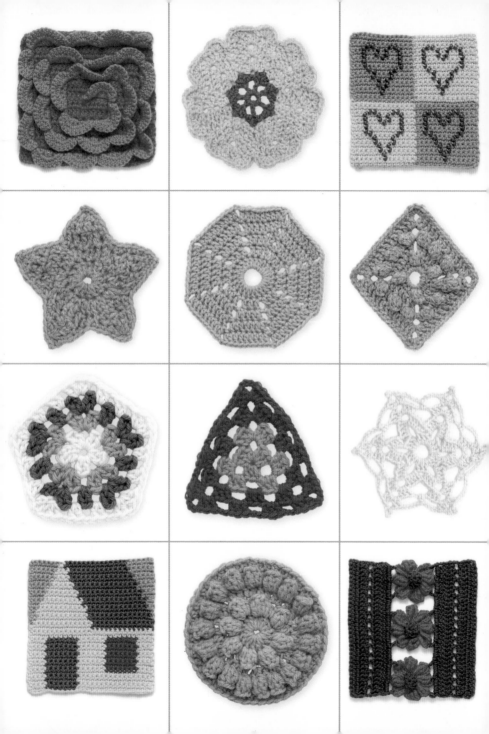

THE CROCHET BLOCK BIBLE

Luise Roberts and Heather Lodinsky

CHARTWELL
BOOKS

A QUARTO BOOK

This edition published in 2015 by
Chartwell Books
an imprint of Book Sales, a division of
Quarto Publishing Group USA Inc.
142 West 36th Street, 4th Floor
New York, New York 10018 USA

ISBN: 978-0-7858-3331-4

Conceived, designed, and produced by
Quarto Publishing plc
The Old Brewery
6 Blundell Street
London N7 9BH

QUAR.CBLB

Technical consultant: Leonie Morgan
Illustrators: Kuo Kang Chen, Coral Mula,
Luise Roberts
Photographers: Paul Forrester, Phil Wilkins
Art director: Caroline Guest
Creative director: Moira Clinch
Publisher: Paul Carslake

The material in this book previously
appeared in *150 Knit & Crochet Motifs*
by Heather Lodinsky and *Crochet Blocks
in a Box* by Luise Roberts.

Color separation by
Cypress Colours (HK) Ltd, Hong Kong
Printed by
Midas Printing International Ltd, China

Contents

About This Book

This book features 100 fabulous crochet blocks, in a range of shapes and sizes, that can be mixed and matched and made into all sorts of projects, from throws and pillows to bags, scarves, and even toys.

Block designs (pages 8–207)

In the main section of the book you will find instructions on how to create 100 different crochet blocks. Organized by shape, and by skill level within each shape, this section contains full instructions, a photograph, and a chart to aid you in the creation of your chosen design.

Techniques (pages 208–223)

This section explains how to fit the different shaped blocks together for your particular project. There is a handy stitch reminder of all the basic crochet stitches used in the book, details of blocking and joining methods, and tips on choosing yarn and calculating how much to buy. At the end you will find a list of the pattern abbreviations and chart symbols.

SIZE OF BLOCKS
The blocks fall into four size categories:

1 Small: 3½–4¾ in. (9–12 cm)
2 Medium: 4¾–6 in. (12–15 cm)
3 Large: 6–7 in. (15–18 cm)
4 Extra large: 7–8¼ in. (18–21 cm)

All of the blocks shown in the photographs have been made using either light worsted-weight yarn on a size 7 (4.5 mm) hook or worsted-weight yarn on a size J (5.5 mm) hook. This information is provided beside the photograph of the block.

The size of the blocks you make yourself will depend on the type of yarn you select and the gauge at which you crochet. See Choosing Yarn (page 209) and Gauge (page 219) for further details.

SKILL LEVEL
You don't need advanced crochet skills to make any of the blocks in this book but some require more concentration than others.

Beginner

Some experience required

More challenging

DIRECTION OF WORK

Worked in rows: This symbol shows that the block has been worked backward and forward in rows.

Worked in rounds: This symbol is used for blocks worked in the round from the center outward.

Some blocks are accompanied by both symbols because part of the pattern is worked in rows and part in rounds.

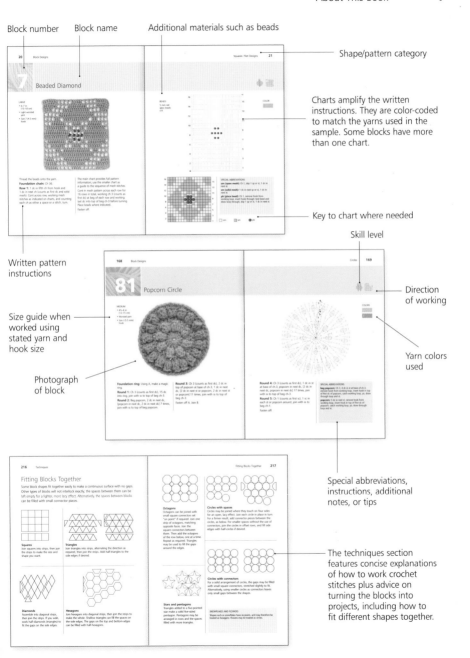

Block number   Block name   Additional materials such as beads

Shape/pattern category

Charts amplify the written instructions. They are color-coded to match the yarns used in the sample. Some blocks have more than one chart.

Key to chart where needed

Skill level

Written pattern instructions

Direction of working

Size guide when worked using stated yarn and hook size

Yarn colors used

Photograph of block

Special abbreviations, instructions, additional notes, or tips

The techniques section features concise explanations of how to work crochet stitches plus advice on turning the blocks into projects, including how to fit different shapes together.

Concentric Squares

LARGE
- 6–7 in.
  (15–18 cm)
- Light worsted yarn
- Size 7 (4.5 mm) hook

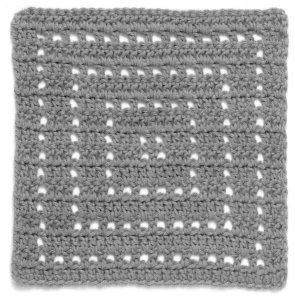

Foundation chain: Ch 36.

Row 1: 1 dc in fifth ch from hook and 1 dc in next ch (counts as first dc and solid mesh). Cont across row, working mesh stitches as indicated on charts, and counting each ch as either a space or a stitch, turn.

The main chart provides full pattern information; use the smaller chart as a guide to the sequence of mesh stitches.

Cont in mesh pattern across each row for 16 rows in total, working ch 3 (counts as first dc) at beg of each row and working last dc into top of beg ch-3 before turning.

Fasten off.

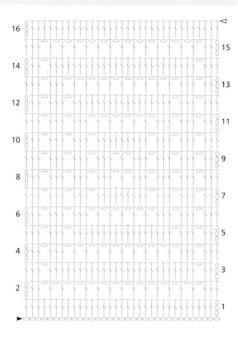

COLOR

SPECIAL ABBREVIATIONS

om (open mesh): Ch 1, skip 1 sp or st, 1 dc in next st.

sm (solid mesh): 1 dc in next sp or st, 1 dc in next st.

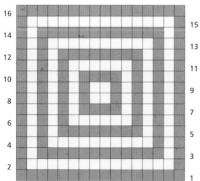

☐ om   ■ sm

2 Spiral Blocks

LARGE

- 6–7 in. (15–18 cm)
- Light worsted yarn
- Size 7 (4.5 mm) hook

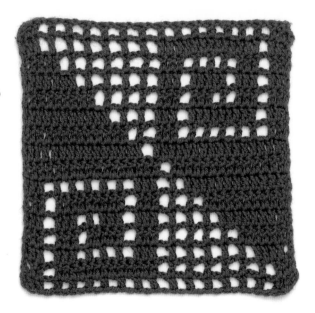

Foundation chain: Ch 36.

Row 1: 1 dc in fifth ch from hook and 1 dc in next ch (counts as first dc and solid mesh). Cont across row, working mesh stitches as indicated on charts, and counting each ch as either a space or a stitch, turn.

The main chart provides full pattern information; use the smaller chart as a guide to the sequence of mesh stitches.

Cont in mesh pattern across each row for 16 rows in total, working ch 3 (counts as first dc) at beg of each row and working last dc into top of beg ch-3 before turning.

Fasten off.

COLOR

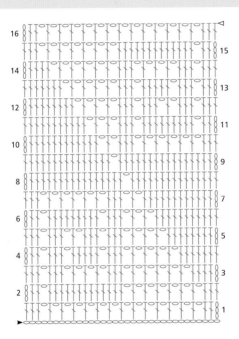

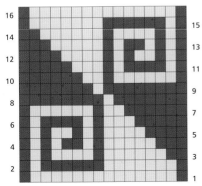

SPECIAL ABBREVIATIONS

om (open mesh): Ch 1, skip 1 sp or st, 1 dc in next st.

sm (solid mesh): 1 dc in next sp or st, 1 dc in next st.

☐ om ■ sm

3 Octagon Rose

LARGE
- 6–7 in. (15–18 cm)
- Light worsted yarn
- Size 7 (4.5 mm) hook

Foundation chain: Ch 37.

Row 1: 1 dc in seventh ch from hook (counts as first dc and open mesh). Cont across row, working mesh stitches as indicated on charts, and counting each ch as either a space or a stitch, turn.

The main chart provides full pattern information; use the smaller chart as a guide to the sequence of mesh stitches.

Cont in mesh pattern across each row for 16 rows in total, working ch 3 (counts as first dc) at beg of each row and working last dc into top of beg ch-3 before turning.

Fasten off.

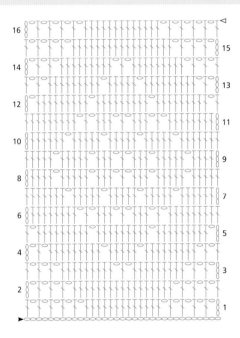

COLOR

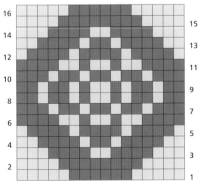

SPECIAL ABBREVIATIONS

om (open mesh): Ch 1, skip 1 sp or st, 1 dc in next st.

sm (solid mesh): 1 dc in next sp or st, 1 dc in next st.

☐ om   ■ sm

4 Runway

LARGE
- 6–7 in. (15–18 cm)
- Light worsted yarn
- Size 7 (4.5 mm) hook

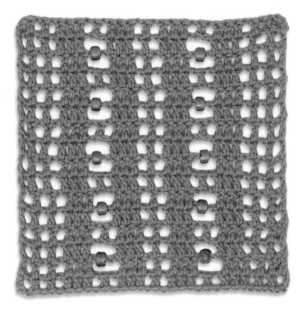

Thread the beads onto the yarn.

Foundation chain: Ch 37.

Row 1: 1 dc in seventh ch from hook (counts as first dc and open mesh). Cont across row, working mesh stitches as indicated on charts, and counting each ch as either a space or a stitch, turn.

The main chart provides full pattern information; use the smaller chart as a guide to the sequence of mesh stitches.

Cont in mesh pattern across each row for 16 rows in total, working ch 3 (counts as first dc) at beg of each row and working last dc into top of beg ch-3 before turning. Place beads where indicated.

Fasten off.

BEADS

6 mm
turquoise
glass beads
x 10

COLOR

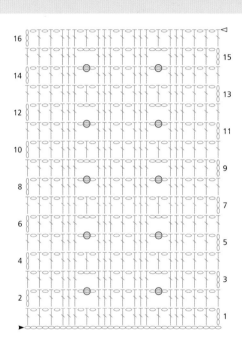

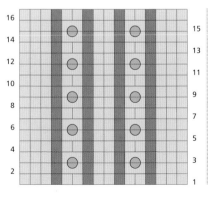

SPECIAL ABBREVIATIONS

om (open mesh): Ch 1, skip 1 sp or st, 1 dc in next st.

sm (solid mesh): 1 dc in next sp or st, 1 dc in next st.

dom (double open mesh): Ch 3, skip 3 ch, 1 dc in next st.

pb (place bead): Ch 3, remove hook from working loop, insert hook through next bead and draw loop through, skip 1 dc, 1 dc in next st.

☐ om   ■ sm   ⊙ pb   ⌐ dom

5

Lacy Heart

LARGE
- 6–7 in.
  (15–18 cm)
- Light worsted yarn
- Size 7 (4.5 mm) hook

Foundation chain: Ch 37.

Row 1: 1 dc in seventh ch from hook (counts as first dc and open mesh). Cont across row, working mesh stitches as indicated on charts, and counting each ch as either a space or a stitch, turn.

The main chart provides full pattern information; use the smaller chart as a guide to the sequence of mesh stitches.

Cont in mesh pattern across each row for 16 rows in total, working ch 3 (counts as first dc) at beg of each row and working last dc into top of beg ch-3 before turning.

Fasten off.

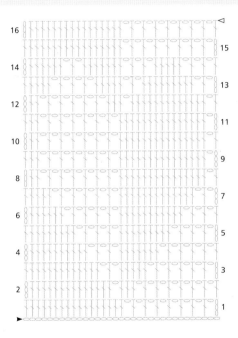

COLOR

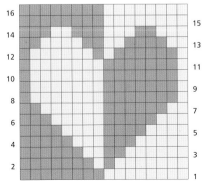

SPECIAL ABBREVIATIONS

om (open mesh): Ch 1, skip 1 sp or st, 1 dc in next st.

sm (solid mesh): 1 dc in next sp or st, 1 dc in next st.

☐ om   ■ sm

6 Lacy Eight-pointed Star

LARGE
- 6–7 in.
  (15–18 cm)
- Light worsted yarn
- Size 7 (4.5 mm) hook

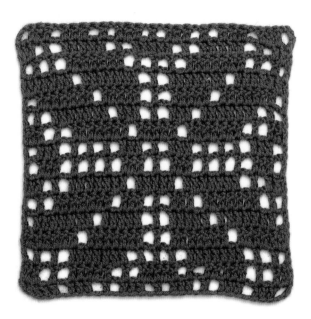

Foundation chain: Ch 37.

Row 1: 1 dc in seventh ch from hook (counts as first dc and open mesh). Cont across row, working mesh stitches as indicated on charts, and counting each ch as either a space or a stitch, turn.

The main chart provides full pattern information; use the smaller chart as a guide to the sequence of mesh stitches.

Cont in mesh pattern across each row for 16 rows in total, working ch 3 (counts as first dc) at beg of each row and working last dc into top of beg ch-3 before turning.

Fasten off.

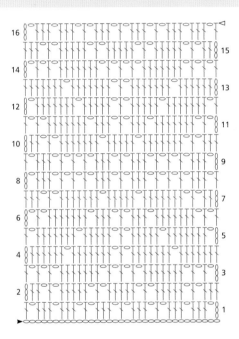

COLOR

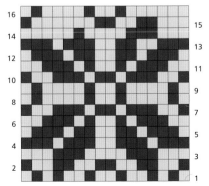

SPECIAL ABBREVIATIONS

om (open mesh): Ch 1, skip 1 sp or st, 1 dc in next st.

sm (solid mesh): 1 dc in next sp or st, 1 dc in next st.

☐ om ■ sm

7

Beaded Diamond

LARGE
- 6–7 in.
  (15–18 cm)
- Light worsted
  yarn
- Size 7 (4.5 mm)
  hook

Thread the beads onto the yarn.

Foundation chain: Ch 36.

Row 1: 1 dc in fifth ch from hook and 1 dc in next ch (counts as first dc and solid mesh). Cont across row, working mesh stitches as indicated on charts, and counting each ch as either a space or a stitch, turn.

The main chart provides full pattern information; use the smaller chart as a guide to the sequence of mesh stitches.

Cont in mesh pattern across each row for 16 rows in total, working ch 3 (counts as first dc) at beg of each row and working last dc into top of beg ch-3 before turning. Place beads where indicated.

Fasten off.

BEADS

5 mm red
glass beads
x 8

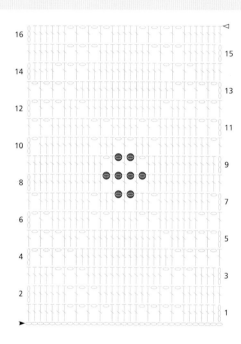

COLOR

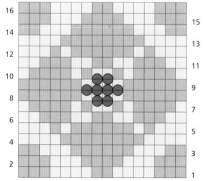

SPECIAL ABBREVIATIONS

om (open mesh): Ch 1, skip 1 sp or st, 1 dc in
next st.

sm (solid mesh): 1 dc in next sp or st, 1 dc in
next st.

pb (place bead): Ch 1, remove hook from
working loop, insert hook through next bead and
draw loop through, skip 1 sp or st, 1 dc in next st.

☐ om   ▨ sm   ● pb

8 Gerbera

LARGE

- 6–7 in.
  (15–18 cm)
- Light worsted yarn
- Size 7 (4.5 mm) hook

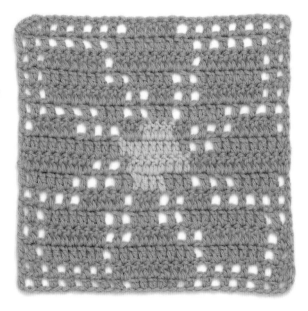

Foundation chain: Using A, ch 37.

Row 1: 1 dc in seventh ch from hook (counts as first dc and open mesh). Cont across row, working mesh stitches as indicated on charts, and counting each ch as either a space or a stitch, turn.

The main chart provides full pattern information; use the smaller chart as a guide to the sequence of mesh stitches.

Cont in mesh pattern across each row for 16 rows in total, working ch 3 (counts as first dc) at beg of each row and working last dc into top of beg ch-3 before turning. Change colors where indicated, weaving in A on reverse of each st worked in B (see page 101).

Fasten off.

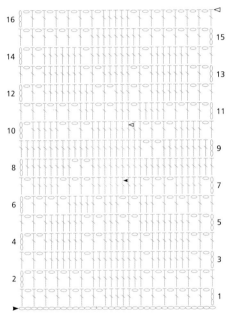

COLORS

A

B

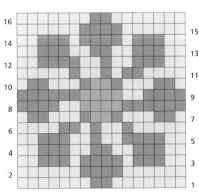

SPECIAL ABBREVIATIONS

om (open mesh): Ch 1, skip 1 sp or st, 1 dc in next st.

sm (solid mesh): 1 dc in next sp or st, 1 dc in next st.

☐ om in A   ■ sm in A   ▨ sm in B

9 Large Leaf

LARGE

- 6–7 in.
  (15–18 cm)
- Light worsted yarn
- Size 7 (4.5 mm) hook

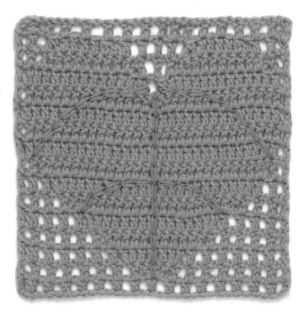

Foundation chain: Using A, ch 37.

Row 1: 1 dc in seventh ch from hook (counts as first dc and open mesh). Cont across row, working mesh stitches as indicated on charts, and counting each ch as either a space or a stitch, turn.

The main chart provides full pattern information; use the smaller chart as a guide to the sequence of mesh stitches.

Cont in mesh pattern across each row for 16 rows in total, working ch 3 (counts as first dc) at beg of each row and working last dc into top of beg ch-3 before turning. The heart is shaped by working increases and decreases leaning to the left or right.

Surface crochet

Using B and referring to main chart and photograph as a guide, work surface chain sts for the leaf veins. Fasten off.

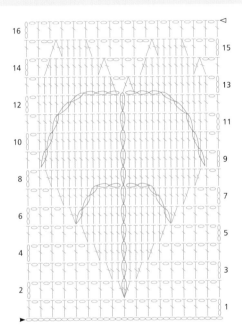

COLORS

A

B

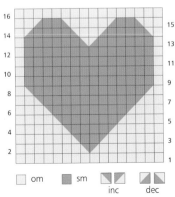

☐ om ■ sm ◨◪ inc ◪◨ dec

SPECIAL ABBREVIATIONS

om (open mesh): Ch 1, skip 1 sp or st, 1 dc in next st.

sm (solid mesh): 1 dc in next sp or st, 1 dc in next st.

inc (increase): For right-leaning increase, skip 1 sp or st, 2 dc in next dc. For left-leaning increase, 1 dc in same st as last dc, skip 1 sp or st, 1 dc in next st.

dec (decrease): For right-leaning decrease, dc2tog working in last st, skip 1 sp or st, and in next st, ch 1. For left-leaning decrease, ch 1, dc2tog over next 2 sts.

Note: The chart at left shows the right side. Reverse the shaping on wrong-side rows—e.g., a left-leaning increase on the front becomes a right-leaning increase on the reverse.

Little Gems

LARGE

- 6–7 in. (15–18 cm)
- Light worsted yarn
- Size 7 (4.5 mm) hook

Foundation chain: Using A, ch 37.

Row 1: 1 dc in seventh ch from hook (counts as first dc and open mesh). Cont across row, working mesh stitches as indicated on charts, and counting each ch as either a space or a stitch, turn.

The main chart provides full pattern information; use the smaller chart as a guide to the sequence of mesh stitches.

Cont in mesh pattern across each row for 16 rows in total, working ch 3 (counts as first dc) at beg of each row and working last dc into top of beg ch-3 before turning. Change colors to work bobbles where indicated.

Fasten off.

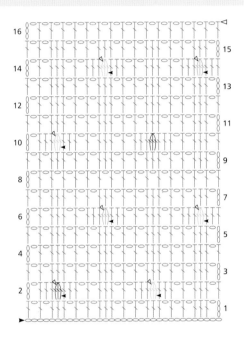

COLORS

A

B

C

D

E

SPECIAL ABBREVIATIONS

om (open mesh): Ch 1, skip 1 sp or st, 1 dc in next st.

sm (solid mesh): 1 dc in next sp or st, 1 dc in next st.

bm (bobble mesh): Using bobble color, *insert hook in next st, yo, draw loop through, yo, draw yarn through 2 loops on hook; rep from * twice more into same st, yo, draw yarn through all 3 loops, fasten off bobble color; using A, 1 dc in next st to complete mesh.

	om in A		sm in A		bm in color indicated

Bamboo

LARGE

- 6–7 in.
  (15–18 cm)
- Light worsted yarn
- Size 7 (4.5 mm) hook

Foundation chain: Ch 37.

Row 1: 1 dc in seventh ch from hook (counts as first dc and open mesh). Cont across row, working mesh stitches as indicated on charts, and counting each ch as either a space or a stitch, turn.

The main chart provides full pattern information; use the smaller chart as a guide to the sequence of mesh stitches.

Cont in mesh pattern across each row for 16 rows in total, working ch 3 (counts as first dc) at beg of each row and working last dc into top of beg ch-3 before turning. Work leaves where indicated.

Fasten off.

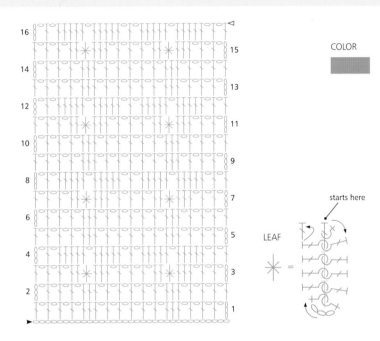

COLOR

starts here

LEAF

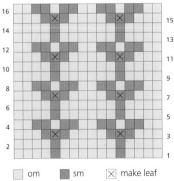

☐ om   ■ sm   ☒ make leaf

SPECIAL ABBREVIATIONS

om (open mesh): Ch 1, skip 1 sp or st, 1 dc in next st.

sm (solid mesh): 1 dc in next sp or st, 1 dc in next st.

make leaf: 1 dc in next st, 1 FPsc and 1 FPdc around same st, 2 FPdc around st on row below, 1 FPdc and 1 FPsc around st on row below that, ch 3. Working around sts just worked, 1 FPsc between sc and dc, 1 FPdc above dc, 1 FPdc between 2 dc on next row, 1 FPdc above dc, 1 FPdc between dc and sc on next row. Working along row in original direction, 1 dc in next st to complete mesh.

12 Layered Spiral

LARGE

- 6–7 in. (15–18 cm)
- Light worsted yarn
- Size 7 (4.5 mm) hook

Foundation chain: Using A, ch 36.

Row 1: 1 dc in fifth ch from hook and 1 dc in next ch (counts as first dc and solid mesh). Cont across row, working mesh stitches as indicated on charts, and counting each ch as either a space or a stitch, turn.

The main chart provides full pattern information; use the smaller chart as a guide to the sequence of mesh stitches. Cont in mesh pattern across each row for 16 rows in total, working ch 3 (counts as first dc) at beg of each row and working last dc into top of beg ch-3 before turning. Fasten off.

Surface crochet

Surface chain: Using B and starting from center, surface crochet around the open mesh spiral, working 2 chains in each open mesh space to end of spiral, turn.

Row 1: Working into surface chain, ch 3 (counts as first dc), 1 dc in next ch, *1 hdc in next ch, 1 sc in next ch, ss in each of next 2 ch, 1 sc in next ch, 1 hdc in next ch, 1 dc in each of next 2 ch; rep from * to end, turn.

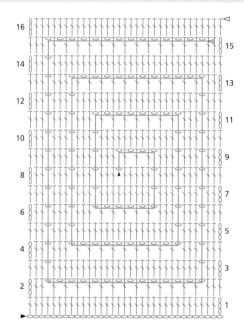

SURFACE CROCHET

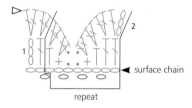

surface chain

repeat

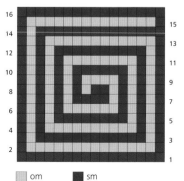

om   sm

Row 2: Ch 3 (counts as first dc), 1 dc in st at base of ch-3, then work 2 dc in each st and 1 ss in each ss of previous row.

Fasten off.

SPECIAL ABBREVIATIONS

om (open mesh): Ch 1, skip 1 sp or st, 1 dc in next st.

sm (solid mesh): 1 dc in next sp or st, 1 dc in next st.

13

Color Dot Square

MEDIUM
- 4¾–6 in. (12–15 cm)
- Worsted yarn
- Size J (5.5 mm) hook

Foundation ring: Using A, ch 4, join with ss to form a ring.

Round 1: Ch 3 (counts as first dc), 11 dc into ring, join with ss to top of beg ch-3. (12 sts)

Round 2: Ch 3 (counts as first dc), 1 dc in st at base of ch-3, 2 dc in each dc around, join with ss to top of beg ch-3. (24 sts)

Fasten off A. Join B.

Round 3: Ch 1, 1 sc in st at base of ch-1, 1 sc in next st, 1 hdc in next st, *3 dc in next st, 1 hdc in next st, 1 sc in each of next 3 sts, 1 hdc in next st; rep from * twice more, 3 dc in next st, 1 hdc in next st, 1 sc in next st, join with ss to first sc. (32 sts)

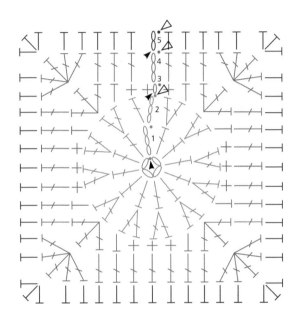

COLORS

A

B

C

Round 4: Ch 3 (counts as first dc), 1 dc in each of next 3 sts, *5 dc in next st, 1 dc in each of next 7 sts; rep from * twice more, 5 dc in next st, 1 dc in each of next 3 sts, join with ss to top of beg ch-3. (48 sts)

Fasten off B. Join C.

Round 5: Ch 2 (counts as first hdc), 1 hdc in each of next 5 sts, *3 hdc in next st, 1 hdc in each of next 11 sts; rep from * twice more, 3 hdc in next st, 1 hdc in each of next 5 sts, join with ss to top of beg ch-2. (56 sts)

Fasten off.

Double Crochet Square

MEDIUM
- 4¾–6 in.
  (12–15 cm)
- Worsted yarn
- Size J (5.5 mm)
  hook

Foundation ring: Ch 4, join with ss to form a ring.

Round 1: Ch 5 (counts as first dc and ch 2), [3 dc into ring, ch 2] 3 times, 2 dc into ring, join with ss to third ch of beg ch-5.

Round 2: Ss in next ch-2 sp, ch 7 (counts as first dc and ch 4), 2 dc in sp at base of ch-7, *1 dc in each of next 3 dc, [2 dc, ch 4, 2 dc] in next ch-2 sp; rep from * twice more, 1 dc in each of next 3 dc, 1 dc in same sp as ch-7, join with ss to third ch of beg ch-7.

COLOR

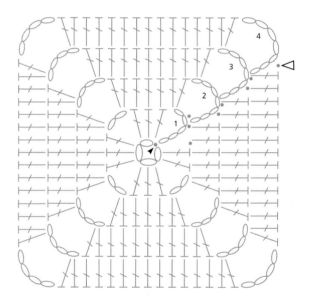

Round 3: Ss in next ch-4 sp, ch 7 (counts as first dc and ch 4), 2 dc in sp at base of ch-7, *1 dc in each of next 7 dc, [2 dc, ch 4, 2 dc] in next ch-4 sp; rep from * twice more, 1 dc in each of next 7 dc, 1 dc in same sp as ch-7, join with ss to third ch of beg ch-7.

Round 4: Ss in next ch-4 sp, ch 7 (counts as first dc and ch 4), 2 dc in sp at base of ch-7, *1 dc in each of next 11 dc, [2 dc, ch 4, 2 dc] in next ch-4 sp; rep from * twice more, 1 dc in each of next 11 dc, 1 dc in same sp as ch-7, join with ss to third ch of beg ch-7.

Fasten off.

15 Woven Stripes

LARGE

- 6–7 in.
  (15–18 cm)
- Light worsted yarn
- Size 7 (4.5 mm) hook

Foundation chain: Using A, ch 31.

Row 1 (RS): Weaving B, 1 dc in fifth ch from hook (counts as first 2 dc), 1 dc in each ch to end, turn. (28 sts)

Row 2: Ch 3 (counts as first dc), weaving B, 1 dc in each st to end, turn.

Rows 3–4: Rep row 2 twice more.

Fasten off B.

Weaving yarns across each row as indicated, continue in dc across each row for 16 rows in total, working ch 3 (counts as first dc) at beg of each row and working last dc into top of beg ch-3 before turning.

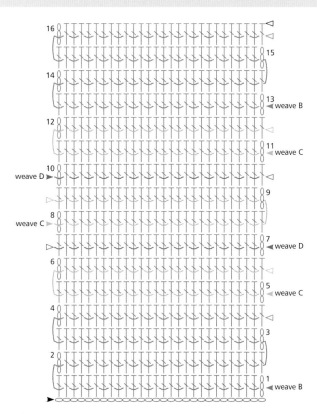

COLORS

A

B

C

D

Weave yarns across each row as follows:
Rows 5–6C, 7D, 8–9C, 10D, 11–12C, 13–16B.

Fasten off.

SPECIAL ABBREVIATION

Weaving: *Bring weaving yarn from back to front, 1 dc in next st, take weaving yarn from front to back, 1 dc in next st; rep from * to end of row, with weaving yarn at front, work last dc in top of beg ch-3.

16 Textured Quarters

LARGE
- 6–7 in. (15–18 cm)
- Light worsted yarn
- Size 7 (4.5 mm) hook

Foundation chain: Ch 26.

Row 1: 1 sc in fourth ch from hook (counts as first 2 sc), 1 sc in each of next 10 ch, *MB in next ch, 1 sc in next ch; rep from * 5 times more, turn.

Row 2: Ch 2 (counts as first sc), 1 sc in each of next 11 sts, *MB in next st, 1 sc in next st; rep from * 5 times more, turn.

Rep row 2, 12 times more.

Row 15: Ch 2 (counts as first sc), 1 sc in each st to end, turn.

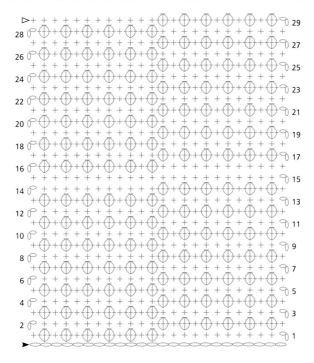

COLOR

Row 16: Ch 2 (counts as first sc), *MB in next st, 1 sc in next st; rep from * 5 times more, 1 sc in each st to end, turn.

Rep row 16, 13 times more.

Fasten off.

SPECIAL ABBREVIATION

MB (make bobble): *Insert hook in next ch or st, yo, draw yarn through, yo, draw through last loop on hook; rep from * twice more in same ch or st, yo, draw through all 4 loops on hook.

Textured Stripes

LARGE
- 6–7 in. (15–18 cm)
- Light worsted yarn
- Size 7 (4.5 mm) hook

Foundation chain: Ch 29.

Row 1: 1 sc in fourth ch from hook (counts as first 2 sc), 1 sc in each ch to end, turn. (27 sts)

Row 2: Ch 2 (counts as first sc), 1 sc in each st to end, turn.

Row 3: Ch 2 (counts as first sc), 1 sc in each of next 2 sts, *1 sc in foundation ch below next st, 1 sc in each of next 3 sts; rep from * 5 times more, turn.

Rows 4–5: Rep row 2 twice more.

Row 6: Ch 2 (counts as first sc), 1 sc in each of next 2 sts, *1 sc in next st 3 rows down, 1 sc in each of next 3 sts; rep from * 5 times more, turn.

Rows 7–12: Rep rows 4–6 twice more.

Row 13: Ch 2 (counts as first sc), 1 sc in each st to end, turn.

Row 14: Ch 3 (counts as first dc), 1 dc in each st to end, turn.

COLOR

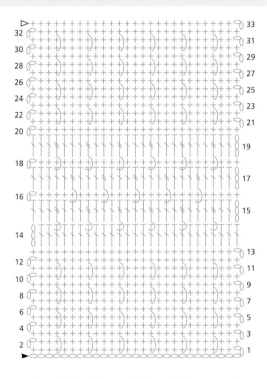

Row 15: Ch 3 (counts as first dc), 1 dc in each of next 2 sts, *FPtr around next st, 1 dc in each of next 3 sts; rep from * 5 times more, turn.

Row 16: Rep row 13.

Row 17: Ch 3 (counts as first dc), 1 dc in each of next 4 sts, *FPtr around next st 2 rows down, 1 dc in each of next 3 sts; rep from * 4 times more, 1 dc in each of next 2 sts, turn.

Row 18: Rep row 13.

Row 19: Ch 3 (counts as first dc), 1 dc in each of next 2 sts, *FPtr around next st 2 rows down, 1 dc in each of next 3 sts; rep from * 5 times more, turn.

Row 20: Rep row 13.

Rows 21–33: Rep rows 4–6, 4 times more, then row 4 again. Fasten off.

18 Tri-color Wheel in Square

LARGE
- 6–7 in.
  (15–18 cm)
- Worsted yarn
- Size J (5.5 mm)
  hook

Foundation ring: Using A, ch 4, join with ss to form a ring.

Round 1: Ch 5 (counts as first dc and ch 2), [1 dc into ring, ch 2] 7 times, join with ss to third ch of beg ch-5.

Round 2: Ss in next ch-2 sp, ch 3 (counts as first dc), 2 dc in sp at base of ch-3, ch 1, [3 dc in next ch-2 sp, ch 1] 7 times, join with ss to top of beg ch-3.

Fasten off A. Join B to next ch-1 sp.

Round 3: Ch 3 (counts as first dc), 2 dc in sp at base of ch-3, ch 1, 3 dc in next ch-1 sp, ch 5, [3 dc in next ch-1 sp, ch 1, 3 dc in next ch-1 sp, ch 5] 3 times, join with ss to top of beg ch 3.

Round 4: Ss between next 2 dc, ch 3 (counts as first dc), 1 dc in next st-sp, 3 dc in next ch-1 sp, 1 dc in each of next 2 st-sp, [3 dc, ch 2, 3 dc] in next ch-5 sp, *1 dc in each of next 2 st-sp, 3 dc in next ch-1 sp, 1 dc in each of next 2 st-sp, [3 dc, ch 2, 3 dc] in next ch-5 sp; rep from * twice more, join with ss to top of beg ch-3.

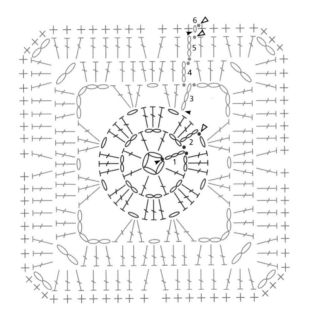

COLORS

A

B

C

Round 5: Ss between last 2 dc, ch 3 (counts as first dc), 1 dc in next st-sp, skip 1 st-sp, 1 dc in each of next 2 st-sp, skip 1 st-sp, 1 dc in each of next 4 st-sp, *[3 dc, ch 2, 3 dc] in next ch-2 sp, 1 dc in each of next 4 st-sp, skip 1 st-sp, 1 dc in each of next 2 st-sp, skip 1 st-sp, 1 dc in each of next 4 st-sp; rep from * twice more, [3 dc, ch 2, 3 dc] in next ch-2 sp, 1 dc in each of next 2 st-sp, join with ss to top of beg ch-3.

Fasten off B. Join C.

Round 6: Ch 1, 1 sc in each dc and 3 sc in each ch-2 sp around, join with ss to first sc. Fasten off.

SPECIAL ABBREVIATION

St-sp: The space between the posts of 2 sts.

19

Tri-color Granny Square

SMALL

- 3½–4¾ in. (9–12 cm)
- Worsted yarn
- Size J (5.5 mm) hook

Foundation ring: Using A, ch 4, join with ss to form a ring.

Round 1: Ch 5 (counts as first dc and ch 2), [3 dc into ring, ch 2] 3 times, 2 dc into ring, join with ss to third ch of beg ch-5.

Fasten off A. Join B to any ch-2 sp.

Round 2: Ch 5 (counts as first dc and ch 2), 3 dc in sp at base of ch-5, *ch 1, skip 3 dc, [3 dc, ch 2, 3 dc] in next ch-2 sp; rep from * twice more, ch 1, skip 3 sts, 2 dc in same sp as ch-5, join with ss to third ch of beg ch-5.

COLORS

A
B
C

Round 3: Ss in next ch-2 sp, ch 5 (counts as first dc and ch 2), 3 dc in sp at base of ch-5, *ch 1, skip 3 dc, 3 dc in next ch-1 sp, ch 1, skip 3 dc, [3 dc, ch 2, 3 dc] in next ch-2 sp; rep from * twice more, ch 1, skip 3 dc, 3 dc in next ch-1 sp, ch 1, skip 3 dc, 2 dc in same sp as ch-5, join with ss to third ch of beg ch-5.

Fasten off B. Join C to any ch-2 sp.

Round 4: Ch 5 (counts as first dc and ch 2), 3 dc in sp at base of ch-5, *[ch 1, skip 3 dc, 3 dc in next ch-1 sp] twice, ch 1, skip 3 dc, [3 dc, ch 2, 3 dc] in next ch-2 sp; rep from * twice more, [ch 1, skip 3 dc, 3 dc in next ch-1 sp] twice, ch 1, skip 3 dc, 2 dc in same sp as ch-5, join with ss to third ch of beg ch-5.

Fasten off.

20

Blue and White Check

LARGE
- 6–7 in. (15–18 cm)
- Light worsted yarn
- Size 7 (4.5 mm) hook

Foundation chain: Using A, ch 17. Without fastening off A, join B and ch 20.

Row 1: 1 dc in fifth ch from hook (counts as first 2 dc), 1 dc in each of next 5 ch, ch 1, skip 1 ch, 1 dc in next ch, ch 1, skip 1 ch, 1 dc in each of next 7 ch, change to A, 1 dc in each of next 7 ch, ch 1, skip 1 ch, 1 dc in next ch, ch 1, skip 1 ch, 1 dc in each ch to end, turn.

Row 2: Ch 3 (counts as first dc), 1 dc in each of next 6 sts, ch 1, skip 1 ch, 1 dc in next st, ch 1, skip 1 ch, 1 dc in each of next 7 sts, change to B, 1 dc in each of next 7 sts, ch 1, skip 1 ch, 1 dc in next st, ch 1, skip 1 ch, 1 dc in each st to end, turn.

Row 3: Ch 3 (counts as first dc), 1 dc in each of next 6 sts, ch 1, skip 1 ch, 1 dc in next st, ch 1, skip 1 ch, 1 dc in each of next 7 sts, change to A, 1 dc in each of next 7 sts, ch 1, skip 1 ch, 1 dc in next st, ch 1, skip 1 ch, 1 dc in each st to end, turn.

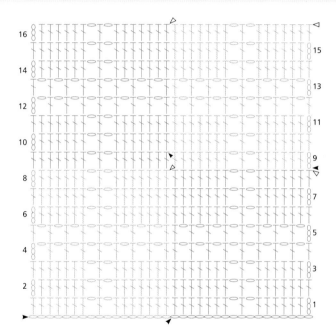

COLORS

A

B

Row 4: Ch 4 (counts as first dc and ch 1), skip 1 st, 1 dc in next st, [ch 1, skip 1 st or ch, 1 dc in next st] 7 times, change to B, 1 dc in next st, [ch 1, skip 1 st or ch, 1 dc in next st] 8 times, turn.

Row 5: Ch 4 (counts as first dc and ch 1), skip first st or ch, 1 dc in next st, [ch 1, skip 1 st or ch, 1 dc in next st] 7 times, change to A, 1 dc in next st, [ch 1, skip 1 st or ch, 1 dc in next st] 8 times, turn.

Rows 6–7: Rep rows 2–3.

Row 8: Rep row 2 but fasten off A and B after completing each section.

Rows 9–16: Continue pattern as set for rows 1–8, alternating A and B to create checked design.

21 Heart Check

LARGE

- 6–7 in. (15–18 cm)
- Light worsted yarn
- Size 7 (4.5 mm) hook

Thread 62 beads onto each yarn.

Foundation chain: Using A, ch 30.

Row 1: 1 sc in fourth ch from hook (counts as first 2 sc), 1 sc in each of next 12 ch. Without breaking off A, join B. Using B, 1 sc in each ch to end, turn. (28 sts)

Row 2: Ch 2 (counts as first sc), 1 sc in each of next 13 sts, change to A, 1 sc in each st to end, turn.

BEADS

4 mm red
glass beads
x 124

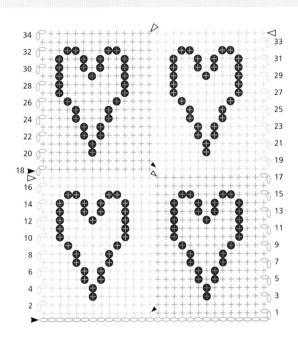

COLORS

A

B

Continue in sc across each row for 34 rows in total, working ch 2 (counts as first sc) at beg of each row and working last sc into top of beg ch-2 before turning. Change colors and place beads as indicated on chart.

Fasten off.

SPECIAL ABBREVIATION

Place beads: On even-numbered (wrong-side) rows, slide bead along yarn to base of hook and then sc into next st. On odd-numbered (right-side) rows, slide bead along yarn to base of hook, insert hook into next st, yo, draw yarn and bead through st, and then complete the sc.

Flower Square

EXTRA LARGE
- 7–8¼ in. (18–21 cm)
- Worsted yarn
- Size J (5.5 mm) hook

Foundation ring: Ch 4, join with ss to form a ring.

Round 1: Ch 1, 12 sc into ring, join with ss to first sc.

Round 2: Beg 2-tr cl, ch 3, 3-tr cl in st at base of beg 2-tr cl, *ch 4, skip 2 sts, [3-tr cl, ch 3, 3-tr cl] in next st; rep from * twice more, ch 4, join with ss to top of beg 2-tr cl.

Round 3: Ch 3 (counts as first dc) *1 dc in top of next cl, [3-dc cl, ch 3, 3-dc cl] in next ch-3 sp, 1 dc in top of next cl, 4 dc in next ch-4 sp; rep from * 3 times more, omitting last dc, join with ss to top of beg ch-3.

Round 4: Ch 3 (counts as first dc), 1 dc in next dc, *1 dc in top of next cl, [3-dc cl, ch 3, 3-dc cl] in next ch-3 sp, 1 dc in top of next cl, 1 dc in each of next 6 sts; rep from * twice more, 1 dc in top of next cl, [3-dc cl, ch 3, 3-dc cl] in next ch-3 sp, 1 dc in top of next cl, 1 dc in each of next 4 sts, join with ss to top of beg ch-3.

COLOR

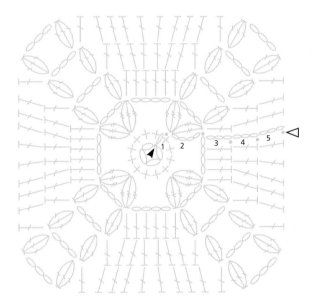

Round 5: Ch 3 (counts as first dc), 1 dc in each of next 2 dc, *1 dc in top of next cl, [3-dc cl, ch 3, 3-dc cl] in next ch-3 sp, 1 dc in top of next cl, 1 dc in each of next 8 sts; rep from * twice more, 1 dc in top of next cl, [3-dc cl, ch 3, 3-dc cl] in next ch-3 sp, 1 dc in top of next cl, 1 dc in each of next 5 sts, join with ss to top of beg ch-3.

Fasten off.

SPECIAL ABBREVIATIONS

beg 2-tr cl (beginning 2 treble crochet cluster): Ch 4, *[yo] twice, insert hook in next st, yo, draw yarn through, [yo, draw through 2 loops on hook] twice; rep from * once more working in same st, yo, draw through all 3 loops on hook.

3-tr cl (3 treble crochet cluster): Work as above from *, but rep from * twice more working in same st, yo, draw through all 4 loops on hook.

3-dc cl (3 double crochet cluster): [Yo, insert hook in next st, yo, draw yarn through, yo, draw through 2 loops on hook] 3 times, yo, draw through all 4 loops on hook.

23 Popcorn Square

MEDIUM
- 4¾–6 in. (12–15 cm)
- Worsted yarn
- Size J (5.5 mm) hook

Foundation ring: Ch 8, join with ss to form a ring.

Round 1: Beg popcorn into ring, [ch 5, popcorn into ring] 3 times, ch 5, join with ss to top of beg popcorn.

Round 2: Ch 3 (counts as first dc), *[2 dc, ch 2, popcorn, ch 2, 2 dc] in next ch-5 sp, 1 dc in top of next popcorn; rep from * twice more, [2 dc, ch 2, popcorn, ch 2, 2 dc] in next ch-5 sp, join with ss to top of beg ch-3.

Round 3: Ch 3 (counts as first dc), 1 dc in each of next 2 dc, *2 dc in next ch-2 sp, ch 2, popcorn in top of next popcorn, ch 2, 2 dc in next ch-2 sp, 1 dc in each of next 5 dc; rep from * twice more, 2 dc in next ch-2 sp, ch 2, popcorn in top of next popcorn, ch 2, 2 dc in next ch-2 sp, 1 dc in each of next 2 dc, join with ss to top of beg ch-3.

Round 4: Ch 3 (counts as first dc), 1 dc in each of next 4 dc, *2 dc in next ch-2 sp, ch 2, popcorn in top of next popcorn, ch 2, 2 dc in next ch-2 sp, 1 dc in each of next 9 dc; rep from * twice more, 2 dc in next ch-2 sp, ch 2, popcorn in top of next popcorn, ch 2, 2 dc in next ch-2 sp, 1 dc

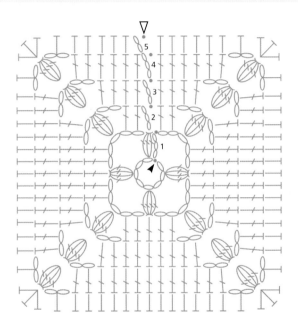

COLOR

in each of next 4 dc, join with ss to top of beg ch-3.

Round 5: Ch 2 (counts as first hdc), 1 hdc in each of next 5 sts, *1 hdc in next ch-2 sp, 3 hdc in top of next popcorn, 1 hdc in next ch-2 sp, 1 hdc in each of next 13 sts; rep from * twice more, 1 hdc in next ch-2 sp, 3 hdc in top of next popcorn, 1 hdc in next ch-2 sp, 1 hdc in each of next 6 sts, join with ss to top of beg ch-2.

Fasten off.

SPECIAL ABBREVIATIONS

beg popcorn: Ch 3, 4 dc into ring, remove hook from working loop, insert hook in top of beg ch-3, catch working loop, yo, draw through loop and st.

popcorn: 5 dc in place indicated, remove hook from working loop, insert hook in top of first dc of popcorn, catch working loop, yo, draw through loop and st.

Off-centered Granny

MEDIUM
- 4¾–6 in. (12–15 cm)
- Worsted yarn
- Size J (5.5 mm) hook

Foundation ring: Using A, ch 4, join with ss to form a ring.

Round 1: Ch 5 (counts as first dc and ch 2), [3 dc into ring, ch 2] 3 times, 2 dc into ring, join with ss to third ch of beg ch-5.

Only two sides of original round are worked until last round. Fasten off A. Join B to any ch-2 sp.

Row 2: Ch 2 (counts as first dc), 2 dc in sp at base of ch-2, ch 1, [3 dc, ch 2, 3 dc] in next ch-2 sp, ch 1, 3 dc in next ch-2 sp, turn.

Row 3: Ch 3 (counts as first dc and ch 1), 3 dc in next ch-1 sp, ch 1, [3 dc, ch 2, 3 dc] in corner ch-2 sp, ch 1, 3 dc in next ch-1 sp, ch 1, 1 dc in last st, turn.

Row 4: Ch 2 (counts as first dc), 2 dc in next ch-1 sp, ch 1, 3 dc in next ch-1 sp, ch 1, [3 dc, ch 2, 3 dc] in corner ch-2 sp, [ch 1, 3 dc in next ch-1 sp] twice.

Fasten off B. Join C.

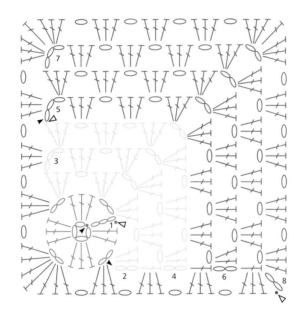

COLORS

A

B

C

Row 5: Ch 3 (counts as first dc and ch 1), [3 dc in next ch-1 sp, ch 1] twice, [3 dc, ch 2, 3 dc] in corner ch-2 sp, [ch 1, 3 dc in next ch-1 sp] twice, ch 1, 1 dc in last st, turn.

Row 6: Ch 2 (counts as first dc), 2 dc in next ch-1 sp, ch 1, [3 dc in next ch-1 sp, ch 1] twice, [3 dc, ch 2, 3 dc] in corner ch-2 sp, [ch 1, 3 dc in next ch-1 sp] 3 times, turn.

Row 7: Ch 3 (counts as first dc and ch 1), [3 dc in next ch-1 sp, ch 1] 3 times, [3 dc, ch 2, 3 dc] in corner ch-2 sp, [ch 1, 3 dc in next ch-1 sp] 3 times, ch 1, 1 dc in last st, turn.

Round 8: Ch 2 (counts as first dc), 3 dc in next ch-1 sp, *[ch 1, 3 dc in next ch-1 sp] 3 times, ch 1, 7 dc in corner ch-2 sp; rep from * once more, [ch 1, 3 dc in beg ch-3 at start of row] twice, ch 1, 3 dc in ch-2 sp of round 1, ch 1, 7 dc in next ch-2 sp, ch 1, 3 dc in next ch-2 sp, [ch 1, 3 dc around post of dc at end of row] 3 times, join with ss to top of beg ch-2.

Fasten off.

25

Raised Squares

LARGE
- **6–7 in.**
  (15–18 cm)
- Light worsted yarn
- Size 7 (4.5 mm) hook

Foundation chain: Using A, ch 31.

Row 1 (RS): 1 dc in fifth ch from hook (counts as first 2 dc), 1 dc in each ch to end, turn. (28 sts)

Row 2: Ch 3 (counts as first dc), 1 dc in each st to end, turn.

Row 3: Ch 3 (counts as first dc), 1 dc in each of next 5 sts, 1 dc tbl in each of next 6 sts, 1 dc in each of next 4 sts, 1 dc tbl in each of next 6 sts, 1 dc in each st to end, turn.

Rows 4–5: Rep row 2 twice more.

Row 6: Ch 3 (counts as first dc), 1 dc in each of next 5 sts, 1 dc tfl in each of next 6 sts, 1 dc in each of next 4 sts, 1 dc tfl in each of next 6 sts, 1 dc in each st to end, turn.

Rows 7–8: Rep row 2 twice more.

Row 9: Rep row 3.

Rows 10–15: Rep rows 4–9.

Row 16: Rep row 2.

Fasten off.

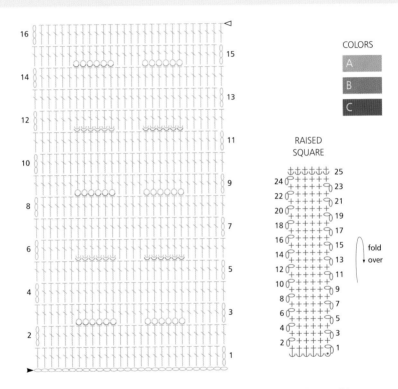

COLORS

A

B

C

RAISED
SQUARE

fold
over

Raised squares

With RS facing, join B with ss tfl at base of row 3, on the right.

Row 1: Ch 2 (counts as first sc), 1 sc tfl in each of next 5 sts, turn. (6 sts)

Row 2: Ch 2 (counts as first sc), 1 sc in each of next 5 sts, turn.

Rep row 2, 22 times more.

Row 25: Fold over and work 1 sc tfl into corresponding st at base of row 3 and 1 sc tfl in each of next 5 sts. Note that this row is worked into the same sts on the main block as row 1 of the raised square.

Fasten off.

Work a raised square into each set of front loops indicated on chart, alternating yarns B and C.

26

Horizontal Weave

LARGE

- 6–7 in. (15–18 cm)
- Light worsted yarn
- Size 7 (4.5 mm) hook

Foundation chain: Using A, ch 31.

Row 1: 1 dc in fifth ch from hook (counts as first 2 dc), 1 dc in each of next 9 ch. Join B, 1 dc in each of next 6 ch, weaving in A on reverse of each st (see page 101). Using A, 1 dc in each ch to end, turn. (28 sts)

Row 2: Ch 3 (counts as first dc), 1 dc in each of next 10 sts. Using B, BPtr around each of next 6 sts. Using A, 1 dc in each st to end, turn.

Row 3: Ch 3 (counts as first dc), 1 dc in each of next 10 sts. Using B, FPtr around

each of next 6 sts, fasten off B. Using A, 1 dc in each st to end, turn.

Row 4: Ch 3 (counts as first dc), 1 dc in each of next 10 sts, 1 dc tfl in each of next 6 sts, 1 dc in each st to end, turn.

Row 5: Ch 3 (counts as first dc), 1 dc in each st to end, turn.

Rep row 5 twice more.

Row 8: Ch 3 (counts as first dc), 1 dc in each of next 6 sts. Join C, 1 dc tfl in each of next 14 sts, weaving in A on reverse. Using A, 1 dc in each st to end, turn.

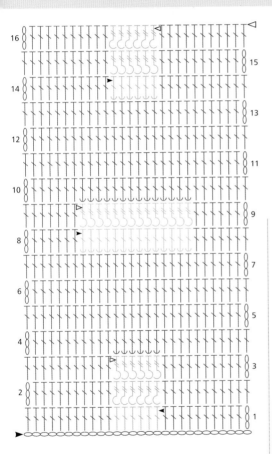

COLORS

A

B

C

Row 10: Ch 3 (counts as first dc), 1 dc in each of next 6 sts, 1 dc tfl in each of next 14 sts, 1 dc in each st to end, turn.

Rep row 5, 3 times more.

Row 14: Ch 3 (counts as first dc), 1 dc in each of next 10 sts. Join B, 1 dc tfl in each of next 6 sts, weaving in A on reverse. Using A, 1 dc in each st to end, turn.

Row 15: Ch 3 (counts as first dc), 1 dc in each of next 10 sts. Using B, FPtr around each of next 6 sts. Using A, 1 dc in each st to end, turn.

Row 16: Ch 3 (counts as first dc), 1 dc in each of next 10 sts. Using B, BPtr around each of next 6 sts, fasten off B. Using A, 1 dc in each st to end, turn.

Fasten off.

Row 9: Ch 3 (counts as first dc), 1 dc in each of next 6 sts. Using C, FPtr around each of next 14 sts, fasten off C. Using A, 1 dc in each st to end, turn.

27

Vertical Weave

LARGE

- 6–7 in. (15–18 cm)
- Light worsted yarn
- Size 7 (4.5 mm) hook

Foundation chain: Ch 31.

Row 1: 1 dc in fifth ch from hook (counts as first 2 dc), 1 dc in each ch to end, turn. (28 sts)

Row 2: Ch 3 (counts as first dc), 1 dc in each of next 10 sts, BPtr around each of next 6 sts, 1 dc in each st to end, turn.

Row 3: Ch 3 (counts as first dc), 1 dc in each of next 10 sts, FPtr around each of next 6 sts, 1 dc in each st to end, turn.

Row 4: Ch 3 (counts as first dc), 1 dc in each of next 10 sts, 1 dc tfl in each of next 6 sts, 1 dc in each st to end, turn.

Row 5: Ch 3 (counts as first dc), 1 dc in each st to end, turn.

Row 6: Ch 3 (counts as first dc), 1 dc in each of next 10 sts, FPtr around each of next 6 sts, 1 dc in each st to end, turn.

Row 7: Rep row 6.

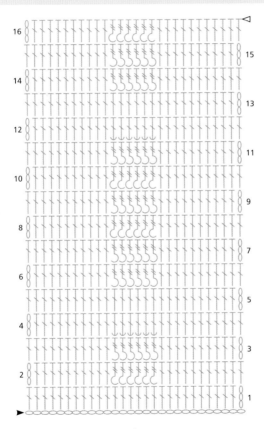

COLOR

Row 8: Ch 3 (counts as first dc), 1 dc in each of next 10 sts, BPtr around each of next 6 sts, 1 dc in each st to end, turn.

Rows 9–10: Rep rows 7–8.

Row 11: Rep row 6.

Rows 12–16: Rep rows 4–8.

Fasten off.

28

All in a Row

LARGE
- 6–7 in. (15–18 cm)
- Light worsted yarn
- Size 7 (4.5 mm) hook

Foundation chain: Using A, ch 31.

Row 1 (WS): 1 dc in fifth ch from hook (counts as first 2 dc), 1 dc in each ch to end, turn. (28 sts)

Row 2: Ch 3 (counts as first dc), 1 dc in each st to end, turn.

To work stripe, remove hook from working loop of A, letting it hang free; do not fasten off. Join stripe color.

Stripe: Using B, ch 2 (counts as first sc), 1 sc tfl in each st to end. Fasten off B.

Row 3: Pick up loop of A at beg of row, ch 3 (counts as first dc), 1 dc tbl in each st at base of stripe to end, turn.

Row 4: Ch 3 (counts as first dc), 1 dc in each st to end, turn.

Using C, work stripe tfl as before.

Rows 5–6: Rep rows 3–4.

Using D, work stripe tfl as before.

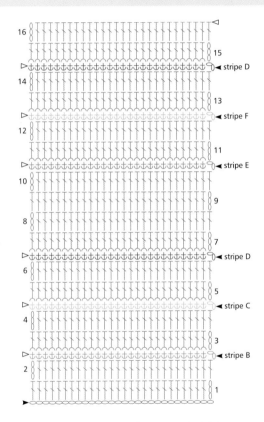

16
15
▷ ◄ stripe D
14
13
▷ ◄ stripe F
12
11
▷ ◄ stripe E
10
9
8
7
▷ ◄ stripe D
6
5
▷ ◄ stripe C
4
3
▷ ◄ stripe B
2
1

COLORS

A
B
C
D
E
F

Rows 7–10: Rep row 3 once more and then row 4, 3 times more.

Using E, work stripe tfl as before.

Rows 11–12: Rep rows 3–4.

Using F, work stripe tfl as before.

Rows 13–14: Rep rows 3–4.

Using D, work stripe tfl as before.

Rows 15–16: Rep rows 3–4.

Fasten off.

29

Nips and Tucks

LARGE

- 6–7 in.
  (15–18 cm)
- Light worsted yarn
- Size 7 (4.5 mm) hook

Foundation chain: Using A, ch 31.

Row 1: 1 dc in fifth ch from hook (counts as first 2 dc), 1 dc in each ch to end, turn. (28 sts)

Row 2: Ch 3 (counts as first dc), 1 dc in each st to end, turn.

Fasten off A. Join B tfl.

Row 3: Ch 3 (counts as first dc), 1 dc tfl in each st to end, turn.

Row 4: Ch 3 (counts as first dc), 1 dc in each st to end, turn.

Row 5 (tuck row): Ch 1, 1 sc tbl in each st 3 rows down to end, turn.

Fasten off B. Join A and rep row 2.

Fasten off A. Join C and rep rows 3–5.

Fasten off C. Join A and rep row 2.

Fasten off A. Join D and rep rows 3–5.

Fasten off D. Join A and rep row 2, 7 times more.

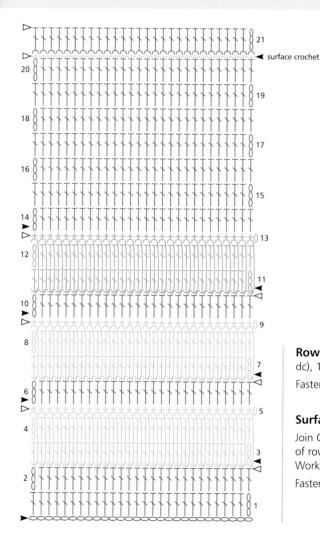

COLORS

| A |
| B |
| C |
| D |

surface crochet

Row 21: Ch 3 (counts as first dc), 1 dc tbl in each st to end.
Fasten off.

Surface crochet

Join C with ss tfl to last st of row 20 (right-hand edge). Work ss tfl in each st to end.
Fasten off.

30 Beaded Star

LARGE
- 6–7 in. (15–18 cm)
- Light worsted yarn
- Size 7 (4.5 mm) hook

Thread the beads onto the yarn.

Foundation chain: Ch 29.

Row 1: 1 sc in fourth ch from hook (counts as first 2 sc), 1 sc in each ch to end, turn. (27 sts)

Row 2: Ch 2 (counts as first sc), 1 sc in each st to end, turn.

BEADS

4 mm silver
metal beads
x 236

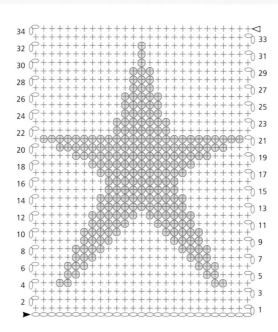

COLOR

Continue in sc across each row for 34 rows in total, working ch 2 (counts as first sc) at beg of each row and working last sc into top of beg ch-2 before turning. Place beads as indicated on chart.

Fasten off.

SPECIAL ABBREVIATION

Place beads: On even-numbered (wrong-side) rows, slide bead along yarn to base of hook and then sc into next st. On odd-numbered (right-side) rows, slide bead along yarn to base of hook, insert hook into next st, yo, draw yarn and bead through st, and then complete the sc.

31

Lotus Flowers

LARGE

- 6–7 in.
  (15–18 cm)
- Light worsted
  yarn
- Size 7 (4.5 mm)
  hook

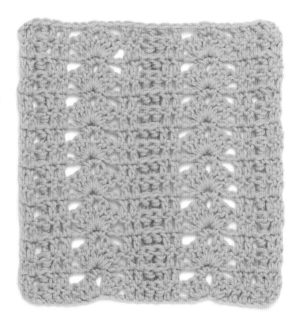

Foundation chain: Ch 31.

Row 1 (WS): 1 dc in fifth ch from hook (counts as first 2 dc), 1 dc in each of next 3 ch, skip 2 ch, 3 dc in next ch, ch 2, 3 dc in next ch, skip 2 ch, 1 dc in each of next 6 ch, skip 2 ch, 3 dc in next ch, ch 2, 3 dc in next ch, skip 2 ch, 1 dc in each ch to end, turn.

Row 2: Ch 3 (counts as first dc), 1 dc in next st, BPtr around next st, 1 dc in each of next 2 sts, ch 2, skip 3 sts, [1 sc, ch 2, 1 sc] in next ch-2 sp, ch 2, skip 3 sts, 1 dc in each of next 2 sts, BPtr around each of next 2 sts, 1 dc in each of next 2 sts, ch 2, skip 3 sts, [1 sc, ch 2, 1 sc] in next ch-2 sp, ch 2, skip 3 sts, 1 dc in each of next 2 sts, BPtr around next st, 1 dc in each of next 2 sts, turn.

Row 3: Ch 3 (counts as first dc), 1 dc in next st, FPtr around next st, 1 dc in each of next 2 sts, skip 1 sc, [3 dc, ch 2, 3 dc] in next ch-2 sp, skip 1 sc, 1 dc in each of next 2 sts, FPtr around each of next 2 sts, 1 dc in each of next 2 sts, skip 1 sc, [3 dc, ch 2, 3 dc] in next ch-2 sp, skip 1 sc, 1 dc in each of next 2 sts, FPtr around next st, 1 dc in each of next 2 sts, turn.

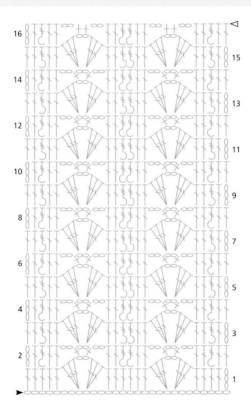

COLOR

Rep rows 2–3, 6 times more.

Row 16: Ch 3 (counts as first dc), 1 dc in next st, BPtr around next st, 1 dc in each of next 2 sts, ch 2, skip 3 sts, 2 sc in next ch-2 sp, ch 2, skip 3 sts, 1 dc in each of next 2 sts, BPtr around each of next 2 sts, 1 dc in each of next 2 sts, ch 2, skip 3 sts, 2 sc in next ch-2 sp, ch 2, skip 3 sts, 1 dc in each of next 2 sts, BPtr around next st, 1 dc in each of next 2 sts.

Fasten off.

32 Lacy Stripes

LARGE
- 6–7 in. (15–18 cm)
- Light worsted yarn
- Size 7 (4.5 mm) hook

Foundation chain: Ch 30.

Row 1: 1 sc in fourth ch from hook (counts as first 2 sc), 1 sc in each ch to end, turn. (28 sts)

Row 2: Ch 2 (counts as first sc), 1 sc in each st to end, turn.

Row 3: Rep row 2.

Row 4: Ch 3 (counts as first dc), 1 dc in st at base of ch-3, *skip 2 sts, [1 dc, ch 1, 1 dc] in next st; rep from * 7 times more, skip 2 sts, 2 dc in top of beg ch-2, turn.

Row 5: Ch 3 (counts as first dc), 1 dc in next st, ch 1, skip 1 st, popcorn in next ch, ch 2, *skip 2 sts, popcorn in next ch, ch 2; rep from * 5 times more, skip 2 sts, popcorn in next ch, ch 1, skip 1 st, 1 dc in each of next 2 sts, turn.

Row 6: Ch 3 (counts as first dc), 1 dc in st at base of ch-3, skip 1 st, 1 dc in next ch, *[1 dc, ch 1, 1 dc] in next ch-2 sp; rep from * 6 times more, 1 dc in next ch-1 sp, ch 1, skip 1 st, 2 dc in last st, turn.

COLOR

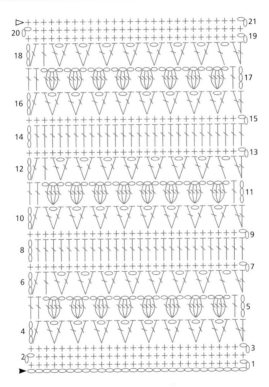

Row 7: Ch 2 (counts as first sc), 1 sc in each st and ch to end, turn.

Row 8: Ch 3 (counts as first dc), 1 dc in each st to end, turn.

Rep rows 3–8, then rows 3–7, and finally rows 2–3. Fasten off.

SPECIAL ABBREVIATION

popcorn: 4 dc in next ch, remove hook from working loop, insert hook in top of first dc of popcorn, catch working loop and draw through to close popcorn.

33

Circles and Bobbles

LARGE
- 6–7 in. (15–18 cm)
- Light worsted yarn
- Size 7 (4.5 mm) hook

Quarter block (top right)

Foundation ring: Using A, make a magic ring.

Round 1: Ch 3 (counts as first dc), 7 dc into ring, join with ss to top of beg ch-3, turn. (8 dc)

Round 2: Ch 2 (counts as first sc), 1 sc in each st around, join with ss to top of beg ch-2, turn.

Fasten off A. Join B.

Round 3: Ch 3 (counts as first dc), 1 dc in st at base of ch-3, 2 dc in each st around, join with ss to top of beg ch-3, turn. (16 dc)

Round 4: Ch 3 (counts as first dc), 1 dc in st at base of ch-3, 2 dc in each st around, join with ss to top of beg ch-3, turn. (32 dc)

Fasten off B. Join C.

Round 5: Ch 2 (counts as first sc), 1 sc in next st, 1 hdc in each of next 2 sts, [2 dc, ch 2, 2 dc] in next st, *1 hdc in each of next 2 sts, 1 sc in each of next 3 sts, 1 hdc in each of next 2 sts, [2 dc, ch 2, 2 dc] in next st;

QUARTER
BLOCK
The colors
shown are
for the top
right quarter

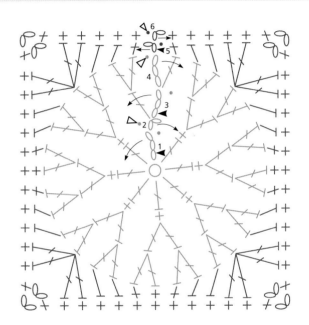

COLORS

A

B

C

D

rep from * twice more, 1 hdc in each of next 2 sts, 1 sc in next st, join with ss to top of beg ch-2, turn.

Round 6: Ch 2 (counts as first sc), 1 sc in each of next 5 sts, [1 sc, ch 2, 1 sc] in next ch-2 sp, *1 sc in each of next 11 sts, [1 sc, ch 2, 1 sc] in next ch-2 sp; rep from * twice more, 1 sc in each of next 5 sts, join with ss to top of beg ch-2.

Fasten off.

Remaining quarter blocks

Work as for top right quarter block but change colors on each round as follows:

Top left: 1–2D, 3–4A, 5–6C.

Bottom left: 1–2A, 3–4D, 5–6C.

Bottom right: 1–2B, 3–4A, 5–6D.

Join the four quarters together using the photograph as reference.

34 Circles Square

LARGE
- 6–7 in. (15–18 cm)
- Worsted yarn
- Size J (5.5 mm) hook

Inner four circles

Foundation chain: Using A, ch 22.

Row 1: Starting in fourth ch from hook, *3 dc in next ch, skip 2 ch, ss in next ch (one quarter circle), skip 2 ch; rep from * twice more, 3 dc in next ch.

Remove hook from working loop, insert hook in last ch worked of foundation chain, catch working loop, and draw through the ch.

Cont along other side of foundation chain, inserting hook in same chains as on row 1.

Round 2: 12 dc in same ch as last 3-dc group of row 1, insert hook through chain and last slip stitch, work ss, *11 dc in ch at base of next 3-dc group, ss in next ss; rep from * twice more, join with ss to last foundation ch. Fasten off A.

Outer 12 circles

Foundation chain: Using B, ch 70.

Row 3: Starting in fourth ch from hook, *3 dc in next ch, skip 2 ch, ss in next ch (one quarter circle), skip 2 ch, 3 dc in next ch,

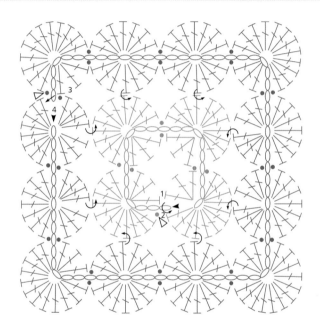

remove hook from working loop, insert hook in fourth dc of upper left circle of round 2, draw working loop though dc, 4 dc in ch at base of last 3-dc group worked (one half circle), skip 2 ch, ss in next ch, skip 2 ch, work another half-circle, joining it to next circle, skip 2 ch, ss, skip 2 ch; rep from * 3 times more.

Remove hook from working loop, insert hook in last ch worked of foundation chain, catch working loop, and draw through the ch.

Cont along other side of foundation chain, inserting hook in same chains as on row 3.

Round 4: 8 dc in same ch as last half circle of row 3, insert hook through chain and last slip stitch, work ss, *7 dc in ch at base of next half circle, ss in next ss, 11 dc in ch at base of next 3-dc group, ss in next ss, 7 dc in ch at base of next 3-dc group, ss in next ss; rep from * twice more, 7 dc in ch at base of next half circle, ss in next ss, 11 dc in ch at base of next 3-dc group, join with ss to last ch of foundation ch.

Fasten off.

Multi-colored Quatrefoil

MEDIUM
- 4¾–6 in. (12–15 cm)
- Worsted yarn
- Size J (5.5 mm) hook

Foundation ring: Using A, ch 8, join with ss to form a ring.

Round 1: Ch 4 (counts as first tr), 5 tr into ring, ch 3, [6 tr into ring, ch 3] 3 times, join with ss to top of beg ch-4.

Round 2: Beg 5-tr cl, ch 5, skip 1 ch, ss in next ch, ch 5, *6-tr cl, ch 5, skip 1 ch, ss in next ch, ch 5; rep from * twice more, join with ss to top of beg 5-tr cl.

Fasten off A. Join B to top of any cluster.

Round 3: Working around next 2 ch-5 sp and next ss, [3 tr, ch 1, 3 tr, ch 2, 3 tr, ch 1, 3 tr] in next ch-3 sp on round 1, *ss in top of next cl on round 2, working around next 2 ch-5 sp and next ss, [3 tr, ch 1, 3 tr, ch 2, 3 tr, ch 1, 3 tr] in next ch-3 sp on round 1; rep from * twice more, join with ss to first ss.

Fasten off B. Join C to any corner ch-2 sp.

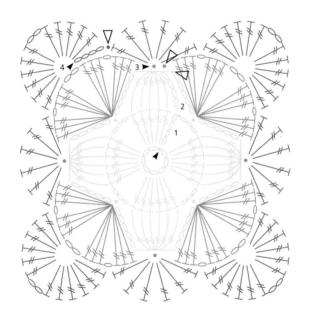

COLORS

A

B

C

Round 4: Ch 4, [5 tr, ch 2, 6 tr] in sp at base of ch-4, skip 6 tr, 6 tr in next ss, *skip 6 tr, [6 tr, ch 2, 6 tr] in next ch-2 sp, skip 6 tr, 6 tr in next ss; rep from * twice more, skip 6 tr, join with ss to beg ch-4.

Fasten off.

SPECIAL ABBREVIATIONS

beg 5-tr cl (beginning 5 treble crochet cluster): Ch 4, *[yo] twice, insert hook in next tr, yo, draw yarn through, [yo, draw through 2 loops on hook] twice; rep from * 4 times more, yo, draw through all 6 loops on hook.

6-tr cl (6 treble crochet cluster): *[Yo] twice, insert hook in next tr, yo, draw yarn through, [yo, draw through 2 loops on hook] twice; rep from * 5 times more, yo, draw through all 7 loops on hook.

36 Concentric Circles

LARGE
- 6–7 in. (15–18 cm)
- Light worsted yarn
- Size 7 (4.5 mm) hook

Foundation chain: Using A, make a magic ring.

Round 1: Ch 3 (counts as first dc), 11 dc into ring, join with ss to top of beg ch-3, turn. (12 dc)

Round 2: Ch 3 (counts as first dc), 1 dc in st at base of ch-3, 2 dc in each st around, join with ss to top of beg ch-3, turn. (24 dc)

Fasten off A. Join B.

Round 3: Ch 3 (counts as first dc), 1 dc in st at base of ch-3, *1 dc in next st, 2 dc in next st; rep from * 10 times more, 1 dc in next st, join with ss to top of beg ch-3, turn. (36 dc)

Round 4: Ch 3 (counts as first dc), 1 dc in st at base of ch-3, *1 dc in each of next 2 sts, 2 dc in next st; rep from * 10 times more, 1 dc in each of next 2 sts, join with ss to top of beg ch-3, turn. (48 dc)

Fasten off B. Join A.

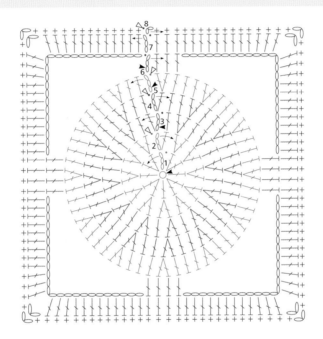

COLORS

A

B

Round 5: Ch 3 (counts as first dc), 1 dc in each of next 2 sts, *2 dc in next st, 1 dc in each of next 3 sts; rep from * 10 times more, 2 dc in next st, join with ss to top of beg ch-3, turn. (60 dc)

Fasten off B. Join A.

Round 6: Ch 3 (counts as first dc), *1 dc in each of next 3 sts, ch 24, skip 11 sts, 1 dc in next st; rep from * twice more, 1 dc in each of next 3 sts, ch 24, skip 11 sts, join with ss to top of beg ch-3, turn.

Round 7: Ch 3 (counts as first dc), *1 dc in each of next 12 ch, ch 2, 1 dc in each of next 12 ch,1 dc in each of next 4 sts; rep from * twice more, 1 dc in each next 12 ch, ch 2, 1 dc in each of next 12 ch, 1 dc in each of next 3 sts, join with ss to top of beg ch-3, turn.

Round 8: Ch 2 (counts as first sc), 1 sc in each of next 15 sts, [1 sc, ch 2, 1 sc] in corner ch-2 sp, *1 sc in each of next 28 sts, [1 sc, ch 2, 1 sc] in corner ch-2 sp; rep from * twice more, 1 sc in each of next 12 sts, join with ss to top of beg ch-2. Fasten off.

37 Flower Trellis

LARGE
- 6–7 in. (15–18 cm)
- Light worsted yarn
- Size 7 (4.5 mm) hook

Flower (make 3)

Foundation ring: Using A, make a magic ring.

Round 1: Ch 3 (counts as first dc), 7 dc into ring, join with ss to top of beg ch-3, turn.

Round 2: Ch 2 (counts as first sc), 1 sc into each st around, join with ss to top of beg ch-2, turn. Fasten off A. Join B.

Round 3: Ch 5 (counts as first dtr of petal), cont to make petal, *ch 5, make petal; rep from * 6 times more. Fasten off.

Trellis

Foundation row: Join A with ss to petal tip of flower 1, ch 6 (counts as 1 dc and ch 3), 1 sc in next petal tip of flower 1, ch 3, 1 dc in next petal tip of flower 1, ch 3, 1 dc in petal tip of flower 2, ch 3, 1 sc in next petal tip of flower 2, ch 3, 1 dc in next petal tip of flower 2, ch 3, 1 dc in petal tip of flower 3, ch 3, 1 sc in next petal tip of flower 3, ch 3, 1 dc in next petal tip of flower 3, turn.

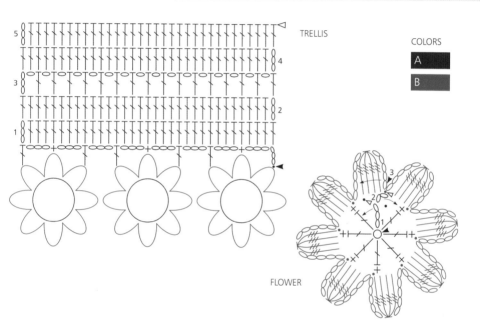

TRELLIS

COLORS

A

B

FLOWER

Row 1: Ch 3 (counts as first dc), *3 dc in next ch-3 sp, 1 dc in next st; rep from * 7 times more, turn. (33 sts)

Row 2: Ch 3 (counts as first dc), 1 dc in each st to end, turn.

Row 3: Ch 4 (counts as first dc and ch 1), skip 1 st, 1 dc in next st, *ch 1, skip 1 st, 1 dc in next st; rep from * to end, turn.

Row 4: Ch 3 (counts as first dc), *1 dc in each ch-sp and st to end, turn.

Row 5: Rep row 2. Fasten off.

Work trellis along other side of flowers in the same way.

Fasten off.

SPECIAL ABBREVIATION

Make petal: *1 dtr in st at base of ch-5, omitting final stage to leave last loop of dtr on hook; rep from * 3 times more, yo and draw through all 5 loops on hook, ch 5, ss in next st.

Multi-colored Granny

LARGE

- 6–7 in.
  (15–18 cm)
- Light worsted
  yarn
- Size 7 (4.5 mm)
  hook

Foundation chain: Using A, ch 6, join with ss to form a ring.

Round 1: Ch 3 (counts as first dc), 2 dc into ring, ch 3, *3 dc into ring, ch 3; rep from * twice more, join with ss to top of beg ch-3.

Fasten off A. Join B to corner ch-3 sp.

Round 2: Ch 3 (counts as first dc), [2 dc, ch 3, 3 dc] in corner sp, ch 1, *[3 dc, ch 3, 3 dc] in next corner sp, ch 1; rep from * twice more, join with ss to top of beg ch-3.

Fasten off B. Join C to corner ch-3 sp.

Round 3: Ch 3 (counts as first dc), [2 dc, ch 3, 3 dc] in corner sp, ch 1, 3 dc in next ch-1 sp, ch 1, *[3 dc, ch 3, 3 dc] in corner sp, ch 1, 3 dc in next ch-1 sp, ch 1; rep from * twice more, join with ss to top of beg ch-3.

Fasten off C. Join D to corner ch-3 sp.

Round 4: Ch 3 (counts as first dc), [2 dc, ch 3, 3 dc] in corner sp, ch 1, [3 dc, ch 1] in each ch-1 sp to corner, *[3 dc, ch 3, 3 dc] in corner sp, ch 1, [3 dc, ch 1] in each ch-1 sp to corner; rep from * twice more, join with ss to top of beg ch-3.

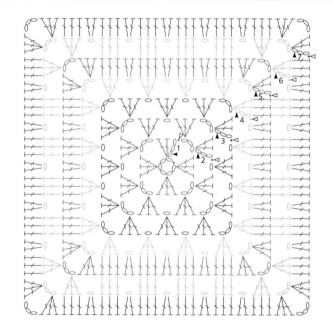

COLORS

A

B

C

D

E

Fasten off D. Join A to corner ch-3 sp.

Round 5: Ch 3 (counts as first dc), [2 dc, ch 3, 3 dc] in corner sp, *1 dc in each of next 3 sts, 2 dc in next ch-1 sp; rep from * twice more, 1 dc in each of next 3 sts, [3 dc, ch 3, 3 dc] in corner sp; cont in patt set, working 1 dc in each st, 2 dc in each ch-1 sp, [3 dc, ch 3, 3 dc] in each corner sp, join with ss to top of beg ch-3.

Fasten off A. Join E to corner ch-3 sp.

Round 6: Ch 3 (counts as first dc) [2 dc, ch 3, 3 dc] in corner sp, ch 1, skip 3 sts,

*1 dc in each of next 3 sts, ch 1, skip 2 sts; rep from * 3 times more, [3 dc, ch 3, 3 dc] in corner sp; cont in patt set, join with ss to top of beg ch-3.

Fasten off E. Join C to corner ch-3 sp.

Round 7: Ch 3 (counts as first dc) [2 dc, ch 3, 3 dc] in corner sp, *1 dc in each of next 3 sts, 2 dc in next ch-1 sp; rep from * 4 times more, 1 dc in each of next 3 sts, [3 dc, ch 3, 3 dc] in corner sp; cont in patt set, join with ss to top of beg ch-3.

Fasten off.

39

Color Swirl Granny

MEDIUM

- 4¾–6 in. (12–15 cm)
- Worsted yarn
- Size J (5.5 mm) hook

Foundation chain: Using A, ch 2.

Round 1: Starting in second ch from hook, [1 sc, 1 hdc, 2 dc] in ch, remove hook from loop A, join B with sc in same ch, [1 hdc, 2 dc] in same ch, remove hook from loop B, join C with sc in same ch, [1 hdc, 2 dc] in same ch, remove hook from loop C, join D with sc in same ch, [1 hdc, 2 dc] in same ch, remove hook from loop D, gently tighten chain into which sts have been worked.

Insert hook into working loops as required.

Round 2: Using A, *2 dc in next sc, 1 dc in next hdc, 2 dc in next dc, 1 dc in next dc, remove hook from loop A; rep from * with colors B, C, and D.

Round 3: Using A, *ch 2, 1 dc in next dc, skip 1 dc, 2 dc in each of next 2 dc, skip 1 dc, 1 dc in next dc, remove hook from loop A; rep from * with colors B, C, and D.

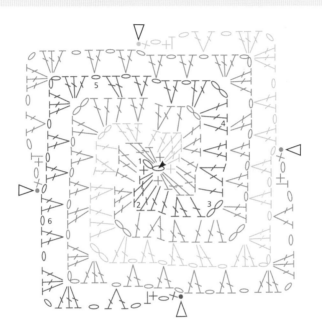

COLORS

A

B

C

D

Round 4: Using A, *[2 dc, ch 2, 2 dc] in next ch-2 sp, [ch 1, skip 1 dc, 2 dc in next dc] 3 times, remove hook from loop A; rep from * with colors B, C, and D.

Round 5: Using A, *ch 1, [3 dc, ch 2, 3 dc] in next ch-2 sp, [ch 1, skip 2 dc, 2 dc in next ch-1 sp] 3 times, remove hook from loop A; rep from * with colors B, C, and D.

Round 6: Using A, *ch 1, 2 dc in next ch-1 sp, ch 1, [3 dc, ch 1, 3 dc] in next ch-2 sp, skip 3 dc, ch 1, 2 dc in next ch-1 sp, skip 2 dc, ch 1, [1 hdc, 1 sc) in next ch-1 sp, skip 2 dc, ch 1, [1 sc, ss] in next ch-1 sp, fasten off A; rep from * with colors B, C, and D.

NOTE
Place working loops not in use onto a split-ring marker or safety pin.

Scales

LARGE
- 6–7 in. (15–18 cm)
- Light worsted yarn
- Size 7 (4.5 mm) hook

Foundation chain: Ch 29.

Row 1 (WS): 1 sc in fourth ch from hook (counts as first 2 sc), 1 sc in each ch to end, turn. (27 sts)

Row 2: Ch 3 (counts as first dc), 1 dc in each of next 2 sts, *make scale in next st, 1 dc in each of next 3 sts; rep from * 5 times more, turn.

Row 3: Ch 2 (counts as first sc), 1 sc in each of next 2 sts, *1 sc around ch-3 of scale, 1 sc in each of next 3 sts; rep from * 5 times more, turn.

Row 4: Ch 3 (counts as first dc), 1 dc in each of next 4 sts, *make scale in next st, 1 dc in each of next 3 sts; rep from * 4 times more, 1 dc in each of next 2 sts, turn.

Row 5: Ch 2 (counts as first sc), 1 sc in each of next 4 sts, *1 sc around ch-3 of scale, 1 sc in each of next 3 sts; rep from * 4 times more, 1 sc in each of next 2 sts, turn.

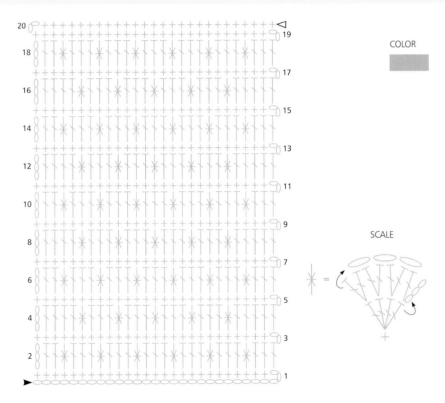

COLOR

SCALE

Rows 6–17: Rep rows 2–5, 3 times more.

Rows 18–19: Rep rows 2–3.

Row 20: Ch 2 (counts as first sc), 1 sc in each st to end.

Fasten off.

SPECIAL ABBREVIATION

Make scale: 4 dc in next st, turn, ch 3 (counts as 1 dc), 1 dc in st at base of ch-3, 2 dc in each st across scale, ch 3, turn.

Rose Garden

LARGE
- 6–7 in.
  (15–18 cm)
- Light worsted
  yarn
- Size 7 (4.5 mm)
  hook

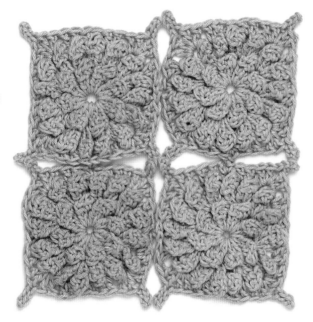

First quarter

Foundation chain: Using A, ch 6, join with ss to form a ring.

Round 1: Ch 3 (counts as first dc of petal), cont to make petal into ring; make petal 7 times more, join with ss to top of beg ch-3. (8 petals)

Round 2: Ch 3 (counts as first dc of petal), cont to make petal into ch-2 sp behind petals on round 1; make petal once more in same sp, make petal twice in each ch-2 sp around, join with ss to top of beg ch-3. (16 petals)

Fasten off A. Join B with ss to next ch-2 sp behind petal.

Round 3: Ch 3 (counts as first dc), 1 dc in sp at base of ch-3, 2 sc in next ch-2 sp, 2 dc in next ch-2 sp, *[2 dc, ch 5, join with ss to first ch of ch-5, 2 dc] in next ch-2 sp, 2 dc in next ch-2 sp, 2 sc in next ch-2 sp, 2 dc in next ch-2 sp; rep from * twice more, [2 dc, ch 5, join with ss to first ch of ch-5, 2 dc] in next ch-2 sp, join with ss to top of beg ch-3.

Fasten off.

COLORS

A

B

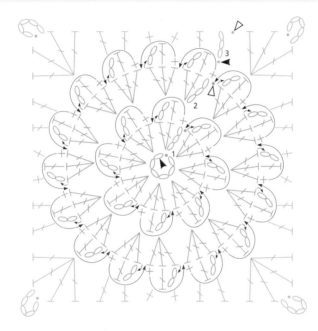

Remaining quarters

Work each remaining quarter in the same way, but on round 3 join to completed quarters by inserting hook between 2 sc on side edge of completed quarter before working second sc of the quarter you are making.

SPECIAL ABBREVIATION

Make petal: 3 dc around ch, turn, ch 2, 1 dc in next st, 1 sc in next st, ch 2, turn.

Note: The final ch-2 of the petal is indicated on the chart by a long curving arrow over the top of each petal. This ch-2 lies behind the petal stitches and takes you across to where you work the 3 dc to start the next petal. The petals on round 2 are worked into this ch-2 sp.

Large Daisy

LARGE

- 6–7 in. (15–18 cm)
- Light worsted yarn
- Size 7 (4.5 mm) hook

Foundation ring: Using A, make a magic ring.

Round 1: Ch 3 (counts as first dc), 11 dc into ring, join with ss to top of beg ch-3, turn. (12 dc)

Round 2: Ch 3 (counts as first dc), 1 dc in st at base of ch-3, 2 dc in each st around, join with ss to top of beg ch-3, turn. (24 dc)

Round 3: Ch 3 (counts as first dc), 1 dc in st at base of ch-3, *1 dc in next st, 2 dc in next st; rep from * 10 times more, 1 dc in next st, join with ss to top of beg ch-3, turn. (36 dc)

Fasten off A. Join B.

Round 4: Ch 3 (counts as first dc), 1 dc in st at base of ch-3, *1 dc tbl in each of next 2 sts, 2 dc tbl in next st; rep from * 10 times more, 1 dc tbl in each of next 2 sts, join with ss to top of beg ch-3, turn. (48 dc)

Round 5: Ch 3 (counts as first dc), [1 dc, ch 2, 2 dc] in st at base of ch-3, *ch 3, skip 3 sts, 1 sc in each of next 5 sts, ch 3, skip 3 sts, [2 dc, ch 2, 2 dc] in next st; rep from * twice more, ch 3, skip 3 sts, 1 sc in each of next 5 sts, ch 3, skip 3 sts, join with ss to top of beg ch-3, turn.

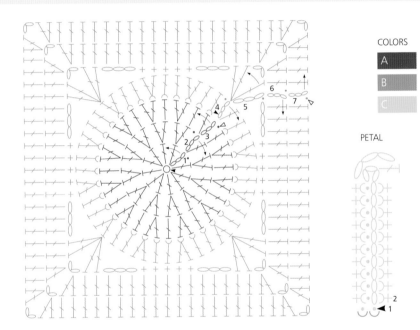

COLORS

A

B

C

PETAL

Round 6: Ch 3 (counts as first dc), *3 dc in next ch-3 sp, 1 dc in each of next 5 sts, 3 dc in next ch-3 sp, 1 dc in each of next 2 sts, [2 dc, ch 2, 2 dc] in corner ch-2 sp, 1 dc in each of next 2 sts; rep from * 3 times more ending 1 dc in last st, join with ss to top of beg ch-3, turn.

Round 7: Ch 3 (counts as first dc), 1 dc in each of next 3 sts, *[2 dc, ch 2, 2 dc] in corner ch-2 sp, 1 dc in each of next 19 sts; rep from * twice more, [2 dc, ch 2, 2 dc] in corner ch-2 sp, 1 dc in each of next 15 sts, join with ss to top of beg ch-3. Fasten off.

Petal

Join C with ss tfl at base of round 4.

Round 1: *Ch 13, skip 3 ch, ss in each loop on reverse of next 10 ch, ss in next front loop at base of round 4; rep from * 35 times more, join with ss to base of first petal.

Round 2: *1 sc tbl in each of next 10 ch, [1 dc, ch 3] in ch-3 sp at end of petal, 1 sc tbl in each of next 10 ss; rep from * 35 times more, join with ss to base of first petal.

Fasten off.

43

Square Deal

LARGE

- 6–7 in. (15–18 cm)
- Light worsted yarn
- Size 7 (4.5 mm) hook

Foundation chain: Using A, ch 30.

Row 1: 1 sc in fourth ch from hook (counts as first 2 sc), 1 sc in each ch to end, turn. (28 sts)

Row 2: Ch 2 (counts as first sc), 1 sc in each st to end, turn.

Continue in sc across each row for 34 rows in total, working ch 2 (counts as first sc) at beg of each row and working last sc into top of beg ch-2 before turning.

Change colors as indicated on charts, joining in a new length of yarn for each area of color. The main chart provides full pattern information; use the smaller chart as a guide to color placement.

Fasten off.

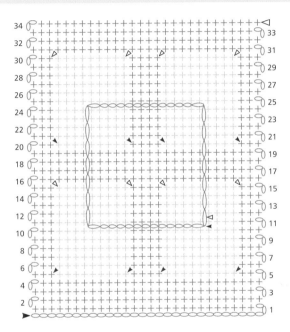

COLORS

A
B
C

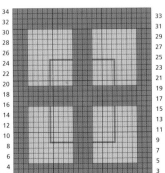

Surface crochet

Using C and referring to charts and photograph as a guide, work a square of surface chain sts around center of block.

Fasten off.

NOTE

See page 95 for advice on working intarsia designs with multiple color changes.

44 Pie Chart

LARGE
- 6–7 in. (15–18 cm)
- Light worsted yarn
- Size 7 (4.5 mm) hook

Foundation chain: Using A, ch 30.

Row 1: 1 sc in fourth ch from hook (counts as first 2 sc), 1 sc in each ch to end, turn. (28 sts)

Row 2: Ch 2 (counts as first sc), 1 sc in each st to end, turn.

Continue in sc across each row for 34 rows in total, working ch 2 (counts as first sc) at beg of each row and working last sc into top of beg ch-2 before turning.

Change colors as indicated on charts, joining in a new length of yarn for each area of color. The main chart provides full pattern information; use the smaller chart as a guide to color placement.

Fasten off.

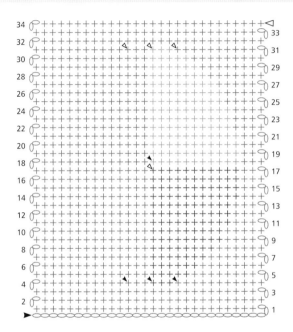

COLORS

A

B

C

D

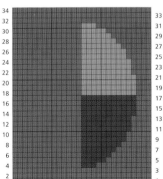

WORKING INTARSIA DESIGNS

- Work each color area using a separate length of yarn, including for unconnected areas of the main background color. To join a new color, omit the final stage of the stitch before the change. Complete the stitch with the new color.

- At each color changeover, loop the new yarn around the old one on the wrong side of the work to prevent holes.

- Take extra care when dealing with all the yarn ends on a piece of intarsia. Carefully weave each end into an area of crochet worked in the same color so that it will not be visible on the right side.

Shoo Fly

LARGE
- 6–7 in. (15–18 cm)
- Light worsted yarn
- Size 7 (4.5 mm) hook

Foundation chain: Using A, ch 31.

Row 1: 1 dc in fifth ch from hook (counts as first 2 dc), 1 dc in each of next 6 ch. Without fastening off A, join B. Using B, 1 dc in each of next 12 ch. Without fastening off B, join a new length of A. Using A, 1 dc in each ch to end, turn. (28 sts)

Row 2: Ch 3 (counts as first dc), 1 dc in each of next 5 sts. Using B, 1 dc in each of next 4 sts. Join a new length of A, 1 dc in each of next 8 sts. Join a new length of B, 1 dc in each of next 4 sts. Using A, 1 dc in each st to end, turn.

Continue in dc across each row for 16 rows in total, working ch 3 (counts as first dc) at beg of each row and working last dc into top of beg ch-3 before turning.

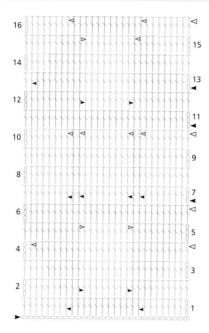

COLORS

A

B

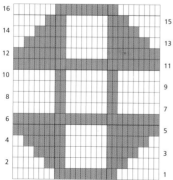

Change colors as indicated on charts, joining a new length of yarn for each area of color. The main chart provides full pattern information; use the smaller chart as a guide to color placement.

Fasten off.

> **NOTE**
>
> See page 95 for advice on working intarsia designs with multiple color changes.

46   Homestead

LARGE

- 6–7 in.
  (15–18 cm)
- Light worsted
  yarn
- Size 7 (4.5 mm)
  hook

Foundation chain: Using A, ch 30.

Row 1: 1 sc in fourth ch from hook (counts as first 2 sc), 1 sc in each of next 15 ch. Without fastening off A, join B. Using B and weaving in A on reverse, 1 sc in each of next 7 ch. Using A, 1 sc in each of next 4 ch, turn. (28 sts)

Row 2: Ch 2 (counts as first sc), 1 sc in each of next 3 sts. Using B and weaving in A on reverse, 1 sc in each of next 7 sts. Using A, 1 sc in each st to end, turn.

Continue in sc across each row for 34 rows in total, working ch 2 (counts as first sc) at beg of each row and working last sc into top of beg ch-2 before turning.

Change colors as indicated on charts, joining in a new length of yarn for each area of colors B, C, and D, and weaving in A on reverse of door and window. The main chart provides full pattern information; use the smaller chart as a guide to color placement.

Fasten off.

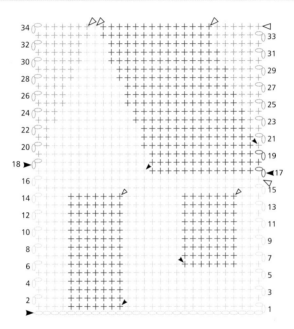

COLORS

A

B

C

D

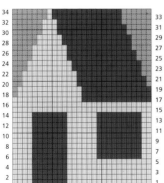

NOTE

See page 95 for advice on working intarsia designs with multiple color changes, and page 101 for guidance on weaving in yarn on the reverse of the block.

47 Fair Isle

LARGE
- 6–7 in. (15–18 cm)
- Light worsted yarn
- Size 7 (4.5 mm) hook

Foundation chain: Using A, ch 29.

Row 1: 1 sc in fourth ch from hook (counts as first 2 sc), 1 sc in each ch to end, turn. (27 sts)

Row 2: Ch 2 (counts as first sc), 1 sc in each st to end, turn.

Continue in sc across each row for 34 rows in total, working ch 2 (counts as first sc) at beg of each row and working last sc into top of beg ch-2 before turning.

Change colors as indicated on charts, weaving in color not being used on reverse of block. The main chart provides full pattern information; use the smaller chart as a guide to color placement.

Fasten off.

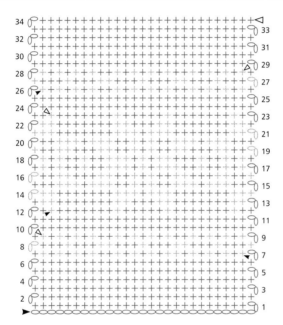

COLORS

A

B

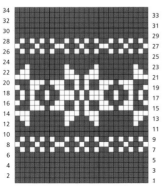

WEAVING IN YARNS

Each of the three bands of Fair Isle pattern require both yarn colors to be carried across the back of the fabric. To avoid unslightly strands of yarn on the reverse of the block, it is important to weave the color not being used into that of the stitch being worked.

To do this, begin working into the next st in the usual way, yo, draw yarn through, wrap yarn not in use around hook from below, wrap working yarn around hook in same direction, return yarn not in use to back of work. Using working yarn, complete the st. This traps the yarn not in use into the st being worked. Repeat this process for every st.

48 Double Crochet Triangle

MEDIUM
• 4³⁄₄–6 in.
  (12–15 cm)
• Worsted yarn
• Size J (5.5 mm)
  hook

Foundation ring: Ch 8, join with ss to form a ring.

Round 1: Ch 3 (counts as first dc), 2 dc into ring, ch 3, [3 dc, ch 3] twice, join with ss to top of beg ch-3.

Round 2: Ch 3 (counts as first dc), 1 dc in each of next 2 sts, *[3 dc, ch 3, 3 dc] in next ch-3 sp, 1 dc in each of next 3 sts; rep from * once more, [3 dc, ch 3, 3 dc] in next ch-3 sp, join with ss to top of beg ch-3.

COLOR

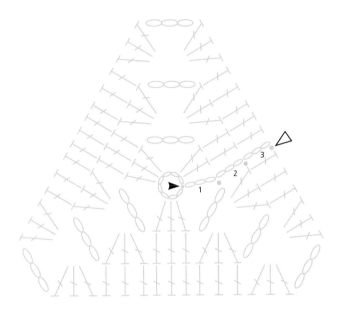

Round 3: Ch 3 (counts as first dc), 1 dc in each of next 5 sts, *[3 dc, ch 3, 3 dc] in next ch-3 sp, 1 dc in each of next 9 sts; rep from * once more, [3 dc, ch 3, 3 dc] in next ch-3 sp, 1 dc in each of next 3 sts, join with ss to top of beg ch-3.

Fasten off.

TIP: CHOOSING COLORS

- Although pastels are perfect for making a project for a baby, any color can be used as long as the yarn is suitable for delicate skin.

- When you have narrowed down your color choices, place skeins of the various color options together in natural daylight to see how well they blend together.

- When in doubt—swatch, swatch, swatch!

49 Solid Granny Triangle

SMALL
- 3½–4¾ in. (9–12 cm)
- Worsted yarn
- Size J (5.5 mm) hook

Foundation ring: Ch 4, join with ss to form a ring.

Round 1: 1 sc into ring, [ch 4, 1 sc into ring] twice, ch 4, join with ss to first sc.

Round 2: Ch 4 (counts as first dc and ch 1), *[2 dc, 1 tr, ch 3, 1 tr, 2 dc] in next ch-4 sp, ch 1; rep from * once more, [2 dc, 1 tr, ch 3, 1 tr, 1 dc] in next ch-4 sp, join with ss to third ch of beg ch-4.

COLOR

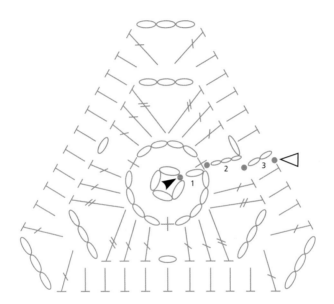

Round 3: Ch 2 (counts as first hdc), 1 hdc in next ch-1 sp, 1 hdc in each of next 3 sts, *[1 hdc, 1 dc, ch 3, 1 dc, 1 hdc] in next ch-3 sp, 1 hdc in each of next 3 sts, 1 hdc in next ch-1 sp, 1 hdc in each of next 3 sts; rep from * once more, [1 hdc, 1 dc, ch 3, 1 dc, 1 hdc] in next ch-3 sp, 1 hdc in each of next 2 sts, join with ss to top of beg ch-2.

Fasten off.

TIP: STORING CROCHET

Apart from dirt and dust, the main enemy of crochet fabrics is direct sunlight, which can cause yarn colors to fade and fibers to weaken. Store all items in a drawer, closet, or other dark, dry, and moth-free place. Check them regularly, refolding the larger items. It is also a good idea to make small cloth sachets filled with dried lavender flowers to tuck into your drawer or closet along with your crochet, as the smell deters moths.

50 Two-tone Granny Triangle

MEDIUM
- 4¾–6 in. (12–15 cm)
- Worsted yarn
- Size J (5.5 mm) hook

Foundation ring: Using A, ch 4, join with ss to form a ring.

Round 1: Ch 5 (counts as first dc and ch 3), [3 dc into ring, ch 3] twice, 2 dc, join with ss to second ch of beg ch-5.

Round 2: Ss in next ch-3 sp, ch 1 [1 sc, ch 5, 3 dc] in same sp, *ch 2, [3 dc, ch 3, 3 dc] in next ch-3 sp; rep from * once more, ch 2, 2 dc in first ch-3 sp, join with ss to second ch of beg ch-5.

Fasten off A. Join B to next ch-3 sp.

COLORS

A

B

Round 3: Ch 1, [1 sc, ch 5, 3 dc] in sp at base of ch-1, *ch 2, 3 dc in next ch-2 sp, ch 2, [3 dc, ch 3, 3 dc] in corner ch-3 sp; rep from * once more, ch 2, 3 dc in next ch-2 sp, ch 2, 2 dc in first ch-3 sp, join with ss to second ch of ch-5.

Round 4: Ss in next ch-3 sp, ch 1, [1 sc, ch 5, 3 dc] in sp at base of ch-1, *[ch 2, 3 dc in next ch-2 sp] twice, ch 2, [3 dc, ch 3, 3 dc] in corner ch-3 sp; rep from * once more, [ch 2, 3 dc in next ch-2 sp] twice, ch 2, 2 dc in first ch-3 sp, join with ss to second ch of ch-5.

Fasten off.

51 Dainty Flower Triangle

LARGE
- 6–7 in.
  (15–18 cm)
- Worsted yarn
- Size J (5.5 mm)
  hook

Foundation ring: Using A, ch 8, join with ss to form a ring.

Round 1: Beg popcorn into ring, ch 3, [popcorn into ring, ch 3] 5 times, join with ss to top of beg ch-3.

Fasten off A. Join B to any ch-3 sp.

Round 2: Ch 3 (counts as first dc), 8 dc in sp at base of ch-3, [ch 4, skip ch-3 sp, 9 dc in next ch-3 sp] twice, ch 4, join with ss to top of beg ch-3.

Round 3: Ch 3 (counts as first dc), 1 dc in st at base of ch-3, *1 dc in each of next 3 dc, [1 dc, 1 tr, ch 3, 1 tr, 1 dc] in next dc, 1 dc in each of next 3 dc, 2 dc in next dc, 1 sc in next ch-4 sp, 2 dc in next dc; rep from * once more, 1 dc in each of next 3 dc, [1 dc, 1 tr, ch 3, 1 tr, 1 dc] in next dc, 1 dc in each of next 3 dc, 2 dc in next dc, 1 sc in next ch-4 sp, join with ss to top of beg ch-3.

COLORS

A

B

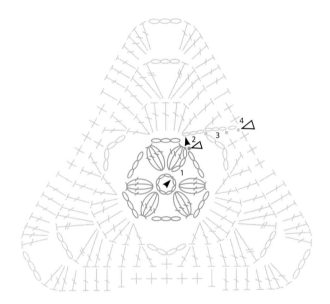

Round 4: Ch 1, 1 sc in st at base of ch-1, 1 sc in next st, *1 hdc in next st, 1 dc in each of next 4 sts, [3 dc, ch 3, 3 dc] in next ch-3 sp, 1 dc in each of next 4 sts, 1 hdc in next st, 1 sc in each of next 5 sts; rep from * once more, 1 hdc in next st, 1 dc in each of next 4 sts, [3 dc, ch 3, 3 dc] in next ch-3 sp, 1 dc in each of next 4 sts, 1 hdc in next st, 1 sc in each of next 3 sts, join with ss to first sc.

Fasten off.

SPECIAL ABBREVIATIONS

beg popcorn: Ch 3, 3 dc into ring, remove hook from working loop, insert hook in top of ch-3, catch working loop and draw through to close popcorn.

popcorn: 4 dc into ring, remove hook from working loop, insert hook in top of first dc of popcorn, catch working loop and draw through to close popcorn.

52

Tri-color Triangle

SMALL
- 3½–4¾ in. (9–12 cm)
- Worsted yarn
- Size J (5.5 mm) hook

Foundation ring: Using A, ch 4, join with ss to form a ring.

Round 1: Ch 1, *[1 sc, 1 hdc, 1 dc, 1 tr, 1 dc, 1 hdc] into ring; rep from * twice more, join with ss to first sc.

Fasten off A. Join B.

Round 2: Ch 4 (counts as first tr), 2 dc in next hdc, 1 hdc in next dc, 1 sc in next tr, 1 hdc in next dc, 2 dc in next hdc, *1 tr in next sc, 2 dc in next hdc, 1 hdc in next dc, 1 sc in next tr, 1 hdc in next dc, 2 dc in next hdc; rep from * once more, join with ss to top of beg ch-4.

Fasten off B. Join C.

COLORS

A

B

C

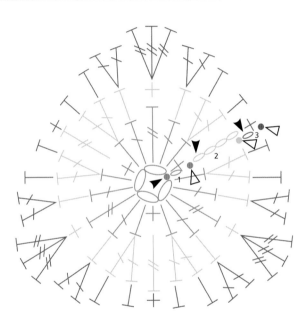

Round 3: Ch 1, 1 sc in st at base of ch-1, *1 hdc in each of next 2 dc, 2 dc in next hdc, 3 tr in next sc (point made), 2 dc in next hdc, 1 hdc in each of next 2 dc, 1 sc in next tr; rep from * once more, 1 hdc in each of next 2 dc, 2 dc in next hdc, 3 tr in next sc, 2 dc in next hdc, 1 hdc in each of next 2 dc, join with ss to first sc.

Fasten off.

TIP: TURNING CORNERS

Whether you are working a triangle, square, diamond, pentagon, hexagon, or octagon, pay particular attention to turning the corners. After every round, also check that you have made the correct number of stitches along each side.

Post Stitch Triangle

LARGE
- 6–7 in. (15–18 cm)
- Worsted yarn
- Size J (5.5 mm) hook

Foundation ring: Ch 8, join with ss to form a ring.

Round 1: Ch 3 (counts as first dc), 4 dc into ring, ch 3, [5 dc into ring, ch 3] twice, join with ss to top of beg ch-3.

Round 2: Ss in next dc, ch 3 (counts as first BPdc), FPdc, BPdc, FPdc, *[2 dc, ch 3, 2 dc] in next ch-3 sp, [FPdc, BPdc] twice, FPdc; rep from * once more, [2 dc, ch 3, 2 dc] in next ch-3 sp, FPdc, join with ss to top of beg ch-3. (9 sts each side)

Round 3: Ch 3 (counts as first BPdc), [FPdc, BPdc] twice, FPdc, *[2 dc, ch 3, 2 dc] in next ch-3 sp, [FPdc, BPdc] 4 times, FPdc; rep from * once more, [2 dc, ch 3, 2 dc] in next ch-3 sp, FPdc, BPdc, FPdc, join with ss to top of beg ch-3. (13 sts each side)

COLOR

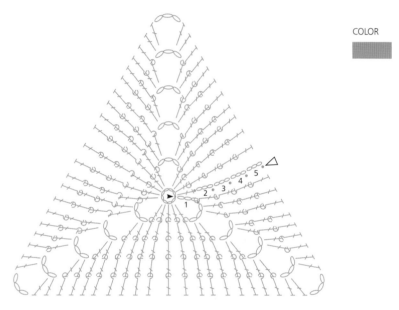

Round 4: Ch 3 (counts as first BPdc), [FPdc, BPdc] 3 times, FPdc, *[2 dc, ch 3, 2 dc] in next ch-3 sp, [FPdc, BPdc] 6 times, FPdc; rep from * once more, [2 dc, ch 3, 2 dc] in next ch-3 sp, [FPdc, BPdc] twice, FPdc, join with ss to top of beg ch-3. (17 sts each side)

Round 5: Ch 3 (counts as first BPdc), [FPdc, BPdc] 4 times, FPdc, *[2 dc, ch 3, 2 dc] in next ch-3 sp, [FPdc, BPdc] 8 times, FPdc; rep from * once more, [2 dc, ch 3, 2 dc] in next ch-3 sp, [FPdc, BPdc] 3 times, FPdc, join with ss to top of beg ch-3. (21 sts each side)

Fasten off.

54

Two-tone Trefoil

MEDIUM
- 4¾–6 in. (12–15 cm)
- Worsted yarn
- Size J (5.5 mm) hook

Foundation ring: Using A, ch 4, join with ss to form a ring.

Round 1: Ch 1, 6 sc into ring, join with ss to first sc.

Round 2: Ch 1, [1 sc, ch 7, 1 sc] in first sc, *1 sc in next sc, [1 sc, ch 7, 1 sc] in next sc; rep from * once more, 1 sc in next sc, join with ss to first sc.

Round 3: Ch 1, skip first sc, [1 sc, 1 hdc, 3 dc, 3 tr, 3 dc, 1 hdc, 1 sc] in next ch-7 sp (leaf made), *skip 1 sc, 1 sc in next sc, skip 1 sc, [1 sc, 1 hdc, 3 dc, 3 tr, 3 dc, 1 hdc, 1 sc) in next ch-7 sp; rep from * once more, skip 1 sc, 1 sc in next sc, join with ss to first sc.

Fasten off A. Join B to second dc of any leaf.

COLORS

A

B

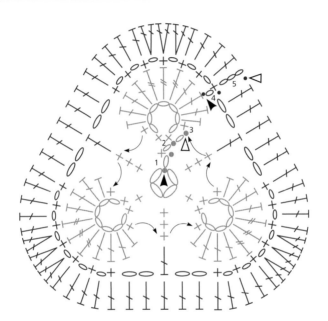

Round 4: Ch 1, 1 sc in st at base of ch-1, [ch 1, 1 sc in next st] 6 times, *ch 2, 1 dc in sc between leaves, ch 2, 1 sc in second dc of next leaf, [ch 1, 1 sc in next st] 6 times; rep from * once more, ch 2, 1 dc in sc between leaves, ch 2, join with ss to first sc.

Round 5: Ch 3 (counts as first dc), *[1 dc in next ch-1 sp, 1 dc in next sc] twice, 2 dc in each of next (ch-1 sp, sc, ch-1 sp), [1 dc in next sc, 1 dc in next ch-1 sp] twice, 1 dc in next sc, 2 dc in next ch-2 sp, 1 dc in next dc, 2 dc in next ch-2 sp, 1 dc in next sc; rep from * twice more, omitting last dc of last rep, join with ss to top of beg ch-3.

Fasten off.

55 Open Trefoil

EXTRA LARGE
- 7–8¼ in. (18–21 cm)
- Worsted yarn
- Size J (5.5 mm) hook

Foundation ring: [Ch 16, ss in first ch] 3 times, to create 3 base loops.

Round 1: In first loop, ch 1 (counts as first sc), 23 sc into loop at base of ch-1, [24 sc into next loop] twice, join with ss to first sc.

Round 2: Ss in each of next 2 sc, ch 5 (counts as first dc and ch 2), skip 1 st, [1 dc in next st, ch 2, skip 1 st] 8 times, 1 dc in next st, skip 5 sts, *[1 dc in next st, ch 2, skip 1 st] 9 times; rep from * once more, join with ss to third ch of beg ch-5.

Round 3: Ch 1, [3 sc in next ch-2 sp] 9 times, 2 sc in sp between next 2 dc; rep from * twice more, join with ss to first sc.

COLOR

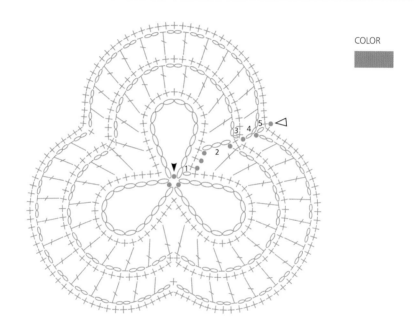

Round 4: Ch 4 (counts as first hdc and ch 2), skip 2 sts, 1 hdc in next st, *[ch 2, skip 1 st, 1 dc in next st] 10 times, ch 2, skip 1 st, 1 hdc in next st, ch 2, skip 3 sc, 1 sc between sts before next sc, skip 3 sts, 1 hdc in next st; rep from * once more, *[ch 2, skip 1 st, 1 dc in next st] 10 times, ch 2, skip 1 st, 1 hdc in next st, ch 2, join with ss to second ch of beg ch-4.

Round 5: Ch 1, 3 sc in each ch-2 sp around, join with ss to beg ch-1.

Fasten off.

56 Tri-color Granny Diamond

MEDIUM
- 4¾–6 in. (12–15 cm)
- Worsted yarn
- Size J (5.5 mm) hook

Foundation ring: Using A, ch 4, join with ss to form a ring.

Round 1: Ch 3 (counts as first dc), 2 dc into ring, ch 2, [3 dc into ring, ch 2] 3 times, join with ss to top of beg ch-3.

Fasten off A. Join B to any ch-2 sp.

Round 2: Ch 3 (counts as first dc), [2 dc, ch 2, 3 dc] in sp at base of ch-3 (right side corner made), ch 1, [2 dc, 1 tr, ch 2, 1 tr, 2 dc] in next ch-2 sp (top corner made), ch 1, [3 dc, ch 2, 3 dc] in next ch-2 sp (left side corner made), ch 1, [3 dc, 1 tr, ch 2, 1 tr, 2 dc] in next ch-2 sp (bottom corner made), ch 1, join with ss to top of beg ch-3.

Fasten off A. Join C to ch-2 sp of right corner.

COLORS

A

B

C

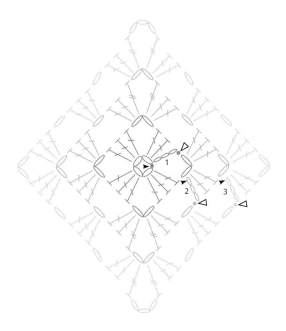

Round 3: Ch 3 (counts as first dc), [2 dc, ch 2, 3 dc] in sp at base of ch-3, ch 1, 3 dc in next ch-1 sp, ch 1, [2 dc, 1 tr, ch 3, 1 tr, 2 dc] in next ch-2 sp (top corner), ch 1, 3 dc in next ch-1 sp, ch 1, [3 dc, ch 2, 3 dc] in next ch-2 sp (left side), ch 1, 3 dc in next ch-1 sp, ch 1, [2 dc, 1 tr, ch 3, 1 tr, 2 dc] in next ch-2 sp (bottom corner), ch 1, 3 dc in next ch-1 sp, ch 1, join with ss to top of beg ch-3.

Fasten off.

TIP: DEALING WITH YARN ENDS

It is important to fasten off yarn ends securely so that they do not unravel during wear or laundering. Try to fasten off as neatly as possible so that the woven in ends do not show through to the front of the work.

57 Geometric Diamond

MEDIUM
- 4¾–6 in. (12–15 cm)
- Worsted yarn
- Size J (5.5 mm) hook

Foundation ring: Ch 4, join with ss to form a ring.

Round 1: Ch 1, [1 sc, 1 hdc, 1 dc, 1 tr, ch 3, 1 tr, 1 dc, 1 hdc] twice into ring, join with ss to beg ch-1.

Round 2: Ch 5 (counts as first dc and ch 2), 1 dc in first sc, 1 dc in each of next 3 sts, [3 dc, ch 4, 3 dc] in next ch-3 sp, 1 dc in each of next 3 sts, [1 dc, ch 2, 1 dc] in next sc, 1 dc in each of next 3 sts, [3 dc, ch 4, 3 dc] in next ch-3 sp, 1 dc in each of next 3 sts, join with ss in third ch of beg ch-5.

COLOR

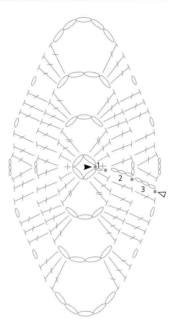

Round 3: Ch 3 (counts first dc), *[1 dc, ch 3, 1 dc] in next ch-2 sp, 1 dc in each of next 2 dc, ch 1, skip 1 dc, 1 dc in each of next 3 dc, ch 1, skip 1 dc, [3 dc, ch 5, 3 dc] in next ch-4 sp, ch 1, skip 1 dc, 1 dc in each of next 3 dc, ch 1, skip 1 dc, 1 dc in each of next 2 dc; rep from * once more, omitting last dc of last rep, join with ss to top of beg ch-3.

Fasten off.

TIP: KEEPING A RECORD

When you have finished making a crochet project, store a small amount of leftover yarn in case you need to make future repairs. Punch a hole in a piece of cardboard and knot several lengths of yarn through the hole. Make a note of the type of yarn and color, as well as details of the project, and attach one of the ball bands to remind you of the yarn composition and any special pressing or washing instructions. File the cards away in a closed box with a lid and store in a cool, dry place.

58 Bobble Diamond

LARGE
- 6–7 in.
  (15–18 cm)
- Worsted yarn
- Size J (5.5 mm)
  hook

Foundation ring: Ch 8, join with ss to form a ring.

Round 1: Ch 1, 16 sc into ring, join with ss to first sc.

Round 2: Beg popcorn in first sc, [ch 1, 1 sc in each of next 3 sc, ch 1, popcorn in next sc] 3 times, ch 1, 1 sc in each of next 3 sc, ch 1, join with ss to top of beg popcorn.

Round 3: Ss in last ch-1 sp, ch 6 (counts as first dc and ch 3), [2 dc in next ch-1 sp, 1 dc in each of next 3 sc, 2 dc in next ch-1 sp, ch 3] 3 times, 2 dc in next ch-1 sp, 1 dc in each of next 3 sc, 1 dc in next ch-1 sp, join with ss to third ch of beg ch-6.

Round 4: Beg popcorn in first st, [1 dc, ch 3, 1 dc] in next ch-3 sp, [popcorn in next dc, 1 dc in each of next 2 dc] twice, popcorn in next dc, [1 tr, ch 3, 1 tr] in next ch-3 sp, [popcorn in next dc, 1 dc in each of next 2 dc] twice, popcorn in next dc, [1 dc, ch 3, 1 dc] in next ch-3 sp, [popcorn in next dc, 1 dc in each of next 2 dc] twice, popcorn in next dc, [1 tr, ch 3, 1 tr] in next ch-3 sp, [popcorn in next dc, 1 dc in each of next 2 dc] twice, join with ss to top of beg popcorn.

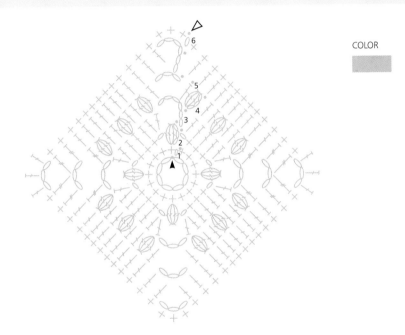

COLOR

Round 5: Ss in first dc, [ss, ch 6 (counts as first dc and ch 3), 2 dc] in next ch-3 sp, 1 dc in each of next 9 sts, [2 tr, ch 3, 2 tr] in next ch-3 sp, 1 dc in each of next 9 sts, [2 dc, ch 3, 2 dc] in next ch-3 sp, 1 dc in each of next 9 sts, [2 tr, ch 3, 2 tr] in next ch-3 sp, 1 dc in each of next 9 sts, 1 dc in next ch-3 sp, join with ss to third ch of beg ch-6.

Round 6: Ch 1, *3 sc in next ch-3 sp, 1 sc in each of next 13 sts, 3 dc in next ch-3 sp, 1 sc in each of next 13 sts; rep from * once more, join with ss to first sc.

Fasten off.

SPECIAL ABBREVIATIONS

beg popcorn: Ch 3, 3 dc in place indicated, remove hook from working loop, insert hook in top of ch-3, catch working loop and draw through to close popcorn.

popcorn: 4 dc in place indicated, remove hook from working loop, insert hook in top of first dc of popcorn, catch working loop and draw through to close popcorn.

59

Granny Pentagon

MEDIUM
- 4¾–6 in. (12–15 cm)
- Worsted yarn
- Size J (5.5 mm) hook

Foundation ring: Using A, ch 5, join with ss to form a ring.

Round 1: Ch 3 (counts as first dc), 1 dc into ring, [ch 1 (counts as corner), 2 dc into ring] 4 times, ch 1, join with ss to top of beg ch-3.

Fasten off A. Join B to any corner ch-1 sp.

Round 2: Ch 3 (counts as first dc), [1 dc, ch 1, 2 dc] in sp at base of ch-3, ch 1, *[2 dc, ch 1 (counts as corner), 2 dc] in next ch-1 sp, ch 1; rep from * 3 times more, join with ss to top of beg ch-3.

Fasten off B. Join C to any corner ch-1 sp.

COLORS

A

B

C

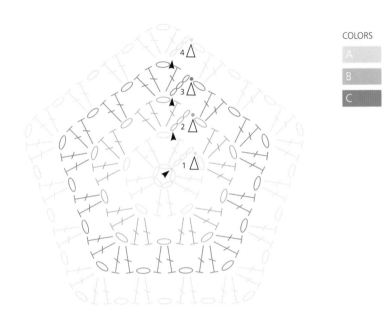

Round 3: Ch 3 (counts as first dc), [1 dc, ch 1 (counts as corner), 2 dc] in sp at base of ch-3, *ch 1, 2 dc in next ch-1 sp, ch 1, [2 dc, ch 1 (counts as corner), 2 dc] in next ch-1 sp; rep from * 3 times more, ch 1, 2 dc in next ch-1 sp, ch 1, join with ss to top of beg ch-3.

Fasten off C. Join A to any corner ch-1 sp.

Round 4: Ch 3 (counts as first dc), [1 dc, ch 1 (counts as corner), 2 dc] in sp at base of ch-3, *[ch 1, 2 dc in next ch-1 sp] twice, ch 1, [2 dc, ch 1 (counts as corner), 2 dc] in next ch-1 sp; rep from * 3 times more, [ch 1, 2 dc in next ch-1 sp] twice, ch 1, join with ss to top of beg ch-3.

Fasten off.

60 Two-tone Pentagon

SMALL

- 3½–4¾ in. (9–12 cm)
- Worsted yarn
- Size J (5.5 mm) hook

Foundation ring: Using A, ch 5, join with ss to form a ring.

Round 1: Ch 2 (counts as first hdc), 2 hdc into ring, [ch 2, 3 hdc into ring] 4 times, ch 2, join with ss to top of beg ch-2.

Round 2: Ss in next hdc, ch 4 (counts as first dc and ch 1), 1 dc in same hdc, [2 dc, ch 2, 2 dc] in next ch-2 sp, skip 1 hdc, *[1 dc, ch 1, 1 dc] in next hdc, [2 dc, ch 2, 2 dc] in next ch-2 sp, skip 1 hdc; rep from * 4 times more, join with ss to third ch of beg ch-4.

Fasten off A. Join B.

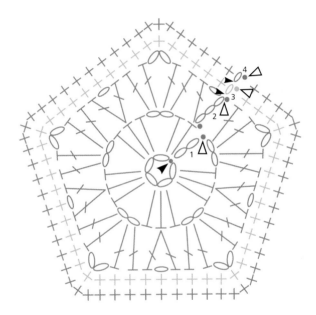

COLORS

A

B

Round 3: Ch 1 (count as first sc), 1 sc in next ch-1 sp, *1 sc in each of next 3 sts, 3 sc into next ch-2 sp, 1 sc in each of next 3 sts, 1 sc in next ch-1 sp; rep from * 4 times more, join with ss to beg ch-1.

Fasten off B. Join A.

Round 4: Ch 1 (counts as first sc), 1 sc in each of next 5 sc, 3 sc in next sc, [1 sc in each of next 9 sc, 3 sc in next sc] 4 times, 1 sc in each of next 3 sc, join with ss to beg ch-1.

Fasten off.

61 Solid Hexagon

MEDIUM
- 4¾–6 in. (12–15 cm)
- Worsted yarn
- Size J (5.5 mm) hook

Foundation ring: Ch 4, join with ss to form a ring.

Round 1: Ch 1 (counts as first sc), 11 sc into ring, join with ss to beg ch-1, turn. (12 sts)

Round 2: Ch 2 (counts as first hdc), [3 hdc in next sc, 1 hdc in next sc] 5 times, 3 hdc in next sc, join with ss to top of beg ch-2, turn. (24 sts)

Round 3: Ch 2 (counts as first hdc), 1 hdc in next hdc, [3 hdc in next hdc, 1 hdc in each of next 3 hdc] 5 times, 3 hdc in next hdc, 1 hdc in next hdc, join with ss to top of beg ch-2, turn. (36 sts)

Round 4: Ch 2 (counts as first hdc), 1 hdc in each of next 2 hdc, [3 hdc in next hdc, 1 hdc in each of next 5 hdc] 5 times, 3 hdc in next hdc, 1 hdc in each of next 2 hdc, join with ss to top of beg ch-2, turn. (48 sts)

COLOR

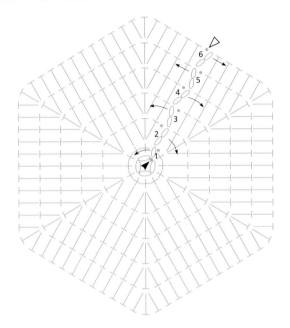

Round 5: Ch 2 (counts as first hdc), 1 hdc in each of next 3 hdc, [3 hdc in next hdc, 1 hdc in each of next 7 hdc] 5 times, 3 hdc in next hdc, 1 hdc in each of next 3 hdc, join with ss to top of beg ch-2, turn. (60 sts)

Round 6: Ch 2 (counts as first hdc), 1 hdc in each of next 4 hdc, [3 hdc in next hdc, 1 hdc in each of next 9 hdc] 5 times, 3 hdc in next hdc, 1 hdc in each of next 4 hdc, join with ss to top of beg ch-2. (72 sts)

Fasten off.

62 Color Dot Hexagon

LARGE
- 6–7 in.
  (15–18 cm)
- Worsted yarn
- Size J (5.5 mm)
  hook

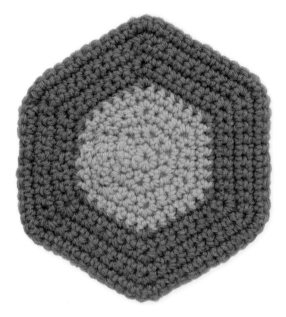

Foundation ring: Using A, ch 4, join with ss to form a ring.

Round 1: Ch 1, 6 sc into ring, join with ss to first sc, turn. (6 sts)

Round 2: Ch 1, 2 sc in each sc around, join with ss to first sc, turn. (12 sts)

Round 3: Ch 1, 1 sc in st at base of ch-1, 3 sc in next sc, [1 sc in next sc, 3 sc in next sc] 5 times, join with ss to first sc, turn. (24 sts)

Round 4: Ch 1, 1 sc in each sc around, join with ss to first sc, turn.

Round 5: Ch 1, 1 sc in st at base of ch-1, 1 sc in next sc, 3 sc in next sc, [1 sc in each of next 3 sc, 3 sc in next sc] 5 times, 1 sc in last sc, join with ss to first sc, turn. (36 sts)

Round 6: Ch 1, 1 sc in each sc around, join with ss to first sc, turn.

Fasten off A. Join B.

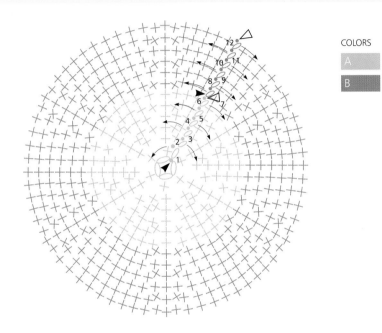

COLORS

A

B

Round 7: Ch 1, 1 sc in st at base of ch-1, 1 sc in each of next 2 sc, 3 sc in next sc, [1 sc in each of next 5 sc, 3 sc in next sc] 5 times, 1 sc in each of next 2 sc, join with ss to first sc, turn. (48 sts)

Round 8: Ch 1, 1 sc in each sc around, join with ss to first sc, turn.

Round 9: Ch 1, 1 sc in st at base of ch-1, 1 sc in each of next 3 sc, 3 sc in next sc, [1 sc in each of next 7 sc, 3 sc in next sc] 5 times, 1 sc in each of last 3 sc, join with ss to first sc, turn. (60 sts)

Round 10: Ch 1, 1 sc in each sc around, join with ss to first sc, turn.

Round 11: Ch 1, 1 sc in each of next 5 sc, 3 sc in next sc, *1 sc in each of next 9 sc, 3 sc in next sc; rep from * 4 times more, 1 sc in each of next 4 sc, join with ss to first sc, turn. (72 sts)

Round 12: Ch 1, 1 sc in each sc around, join with ss to first sc.

Fasten off.

63 Granny Hexagon

LARGE
- 6–7 in. (15–18 cm)
- Worsted yarn
- Size J (5.5 mm) hook

Foundation ring: Using A, ch 6, join with ss to form a ring.

Round 1: Ch 3 (counts as first dc), dc2tog into ring, [ch 3, dc3tog into ring] 5 times, ch 3, join with ss to top of beg ch-3.

Round 2: Ss in next ch-3 sp, ch 3 (counts as first dc), [dc2tog, ch 3, dc3tog] in sp at base of ch-3, [ch 3, (dc3tog, ch 3, dc3tog) in next ch-3 sp] 5 times, ch 3, join with ss to top of beg ch-3.

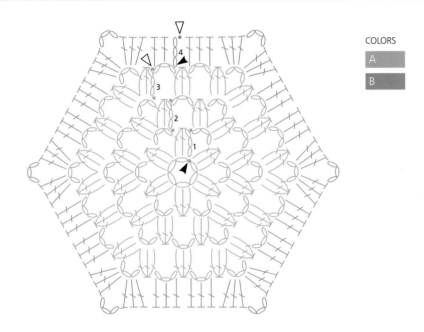

COLORS

A

B

Round 3: Ss in next ch-3 sp, ch 3 (counts as first dc), [dc2tog, ch 3, dc3tog] in sp at base of ch-3, [ch 3, dc3tog in next ch-3 sp, ch 3, (dc3tog, ch 3, dc3tog) in next ch-3 sp] 5 times, ch 3, dc3tog in next ch-3 sp, ch 3, join with ss to top of beg ch-3.

Fasten off A. Join B to last ch-3 sp.

Round 4: Ch 3 (counts as first dc), 2 dc in sp at base of ch-3, [(3 dc, ch 2, 3 dc) in next ch-3 sp, (3 dc in next ch-3 sp) twice] 5 times, [3 dc, ch 2, 3 dc] in next ch-3 sp, 3 dc in next ch-3 sp, join with ss to top of beg ch-3.

Fasten off.

64 Classic Hexagon

EXTRA LARGE
- 7–8¼ in. (18–21 cm)
- Worsted yarn
- Size J (5.5 mm) hook

Foundation ring: Using A, ch 6, join with ss to form a ring.

Round 1: Ch 4 (counts as first dc and ch 1), [1 dc into ring, ch 1] 11 times, join with ss to third ch of beg ch-4.

Round 2: Ch 3 (counts as first dc), 2 dc in next ch-1 sp, 1 dc in next dc, ch 2, [1 dc in next dc, 2 dc in next ch-1 sp, 1 dc in next dc, ch 2] 5 times, join with ss to top of beg ch-3.

Round 3: Ch 3 (counts as first dc), 1 dc in st at base of ch-3, 1 dc in each of next 2 dc, 2 dc in next dc, ch 2, [2 dc in next dc, 1 dc in each of next 2 dc, 2 dc in next dc, ch 2] 5 times, join with ss to top of beg ch-3. Fasten off A. Join B.

Round 4: Ch 3 (counts as first dc), 1 dc in st at base of ch-3, 1 dc in each of next 4 dc, 2 dc in next dc, ch 2, [2 dc in next dc, 1 dc in each of next 4 dc, 2 dc in next dc, ch 2] 5 times, join with ss to top of beg ch-3.

Round 5: Ch 3 (counts as first dc), 1 dc in each of next 7 dc, [ch 3, 1 sc in next ch-2 sp, ch 3, 1 dc in each of next 8 dc] 5 times,

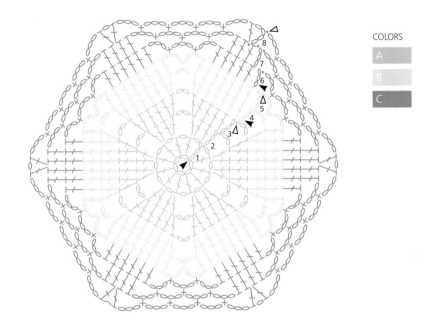

COLORS

A

B

C

ch 3, 1 sc in next ch-2 sp, ch 3, join with ss to top of beg ch-3. Fasten off B. Join C.

Round 6: Ss in next dc, ch 3 (counts as first dc), 1 dc in each of next 5 dc, *ch 3, [1 sc in next ch-3 sp, ch 3] twice, skip 1 dc, 1 dc in each of next 6 dc; rep from * 4 times more, ch 3, [1 sc in next ch-3 sp, ch 3] twice, join with ss to top of beg ch-3.

Round 7: Ss in next dc, ch 3 (counts as first dc), 1 dc in each of next 3 dc, *ch 3, [1 sc in next ch-3 sp, ch 3] 3 times, skip 1 dc, 1 dc in each of next 4 dc; rep from * 4 times more,

ch 3, [1 sc in next ch-3 sp, ch 3] 3 times, join with ss to top of beg ch-3.

Round 8: Ss in st-sp between second and third dc of group, ch 4 (counts as first dc and ch 1), 1 dc in st at base of ch-4, *ch 3, [1 sc in next ch-3 sp, ch 3] 4 times, [1 dc, ch 1, 1 dc] in st-sp between second and third dc of next 4-dc group; rep from * 4 times more, ch 3, [1 sc in next ch-3 sp, ch 3] 4 times, join with ss to third ch of beg ch-4.

Fasten off.

65 Swirl Hexagon

LARGE
- 6–7 in.
  (15–18 cm)
- Worsted yarn
- Size J (5.5 mm)
  hook

Foundation ring: Ch 4, join with ss to form a ring.

Round 1: Beg 2-dc cl into ring, [ch 2, 3-dc cl into ring] 5 times, ch 2, join with ss to top of beg 2-dc cl.

Round 2: [Ch 4, 1 sc in top of next cl] 6 times.

Round 3: [Ch 4, 2 sc in next ch-4 sp, 1 sc in next sc] 6 times.

Round 4: [Ch 4, 2 sc in next ch-4 sp, 1 sc in each of next 2 sc, skip 1 sc] 6 times.

Round 5: [Ch 4, 2 sc in next ch-4 sp, 1 sc in each of next 3 sc, skip 1 sc] 6 times.

Round 6: [Ch 4, 2 sc in next ch-4 sp, 1 sc in each of next 4 sc, skip 1 sc] 6 times.

Round 7: [Ch 4, 2 sc in next ch-4 sp, 1 sc in each of next 5 sc, skip 1 sc] 6 times.

COLOR

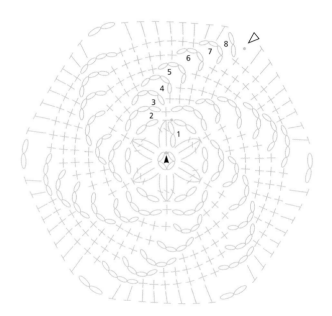

Round 8: [Ch 2, 2 hdc in next ch-4 sp,
1 hdc in each of next 6 sc, skip 1 sc] 6 times,
join with ss to top of beg ch-2.

Fasten off.

NOTE
Mark beginning of round with a detachable marker
or safety pin and move the marker up as you work.

SPECIAL ABBREVIATIONS

**beg 2-dc cl (beginning 2 double crochet
cluster):** Ch 2, [yo, insert hook into ring, yo, draw
yarn through, yo, draw through 2 loops on hook]
twice, yo, draw through all 3 loops on hook.

3-dc cl (3 double crochet cluster): [Yo, insert
hook into ring, yo, draw yarn through, yo, draw
through 2 loops on hook] 3 times, yo, draw
through all 4 loops on hook.

66 Wheel Hexagon

MEDIUM
- 4¾–6 in. (12–15 cm)
- Worsted yarn
- Size J (5.5 mm) hook

Foundation ring: Ch 6, join with ss to form a ring.

Round 1: Ch 6 (counts as first tr and ch 2), [1 tr into ring, ch 2] 11 times, join with ss to fourth ch of beg ch-6.

Round 2: Ss in next ch-2 sp, ch 3 (counts as first dc), [1 dc, ch 2, 2 dc] in sp at base of ch-3, [3 dc in next ch-2 sp, (2 dc, ch 2, 2 dc) in next ch-2 sp] 5 times, 3 dc in next ch-2 sp, join with ss to top of beg ch-3.

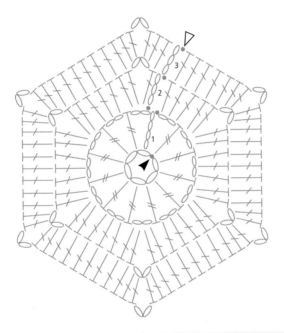

COLOR

Round 3: Ch 3 (counts as first dc), 1 dc in next dc, [(2 dc, ch 1, 2 dc) in next ch-2 sp, 1 dc in each of next 7 dc] 5 times, [2 dc, ch 1, 2 dc] in next ch-2 sp, 1 dc in each of next 5 dc, join with ss to top of beg ch-3.

Fasten off.

TIP: LAUNDERING CROCHET

When laundering crochet, always follow the washing and pressing instructions given on the yarn ball band. If the yarn is machine washable, put the item into a zippered mesh laundry bag to keep it from stretching and snagging during the wash cycle. For items that are not machine washable, handwash in hot water with a mild, detergent-free cleaning agent. Most purpose-made wool or fabric shampoos are ideal, but check that the one you choose does not contain optical brighteners, which will cause yarn colors to fade.

67 Double Crochet Spoke Octagon

LARGE
- 6–7 in. (15–18 cm)
- Worsted yarn
- Size J (5.5 mm) hook

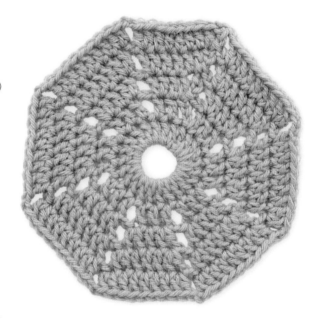

Foundation ring: Ch 4, join with ss to form a ring.

Round 1: Ch 3 (counts as first dc), 23 dc into ring, join with ss to top of beg ch-3.

Round 2: Ch 3 (counts as first dc), 1 dc in each of next 2 dc, [ch 2, 1 dc in each of next 3 dc] 7 times, ch 2, join with ss to top of beg ch-3.

Round 3: Ch 3 (counts as first dc), 1 dc in st at base of ch-3, 1 dc in next dc, 2 dc in next dc, [ch 2, 2 dc in next dc, 1 dc in next dc, 2 dc in next dc] 7 times, ch 2, join with ss to top of beg ch-3.

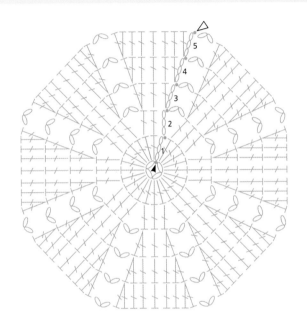

COLOR

Round 4: Ch 3 (counts as first dc), 1 dc in st at base of ch-3, 1 dc in each of next 3 dc, 2 dc in next dc, [ch 2, 2 dc in next dc, 1 dc in each of next 3 dc, 2 dc in next dc] 7 times, ch 2, join with ss to top of beg ch-3.

Round 5: Ch 3 (counts as first dc), 1 dc in st at base of ch-3, 1 dc in each of next 5 dc, 2 dc in next dc, [ch 2, 2 dc in next dc, 1 dc in each of next 5 dc, 2 dc in next dc] 7 times, ch 2, join with ss to top of beg ch-3.

Fasten off.

68 Multi-colored Octagon

MEDIUM
- 4¾–6 in. (12–15 cm)
- Worsted yarn
- Size J (5.5 mm) hook

Foundation ring: Using A, ch 4, join with ss to form a ring.

Round 1: Ch 3 (counts as first dc), 15 dc into ring, join with ss to top of beg ch-3. (16 sts)

Fasten off A. Join B.

Round 2: Ch 3 (counts as first dc), 2 dc in st at base of ch-3, 1 dc in next dc, [3 dc in next dc, 1 dc in next dc] 7 times, join with ss to top of beg ch-3. (32 sts)

Fasten off B. Join C.

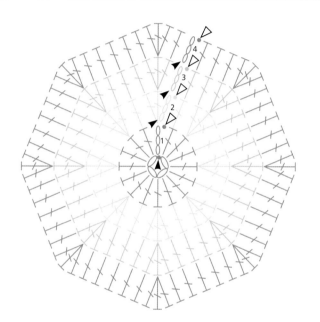

COLORS

A

B

C

Round 3: Ch 3 (counts as first dc), [3 dc in next dc, 1 dc in each of next 3 dc] 7 times, 3 dc in next dc, 1 dc in each of next 2 dc, join with ss to top of beg ch-3. (48 sts)

Fasten off C. Join A.

Round 4: Ch 3 (counts as first dc), 1 dc in next dc, [3 dc in next dc, 1 dc in each of next 5 dc] 7 times, 3 dc in next dc, 1 dc in each of next 3 dc, join with ss to top of beg ch-3. (64 sts)

Fasten off.

69 Octagon Granny

LARGE
- 6–7 in. (15–18 cm)
- Worsted yarn
- Size J (5.5 mm) hook

Foundation ring: Using A, ch 5, join with ss to form a ring.

Round 1: Ch 3 (counts as first dc), 2 dc into ring, ch 1, [3 dc into ring, ch 1] 3 times, join with ss to top of beg ch-3.

Fasten off A. Join B to any ch-1 sp.

Round 2: Ch 3 (counts as first dc), [2 dc, ch 1, 3 dc] in sp at base of ch-3, ch 1, *[3 dc, ch 1, 3 dc] in next ch-1 sp, ch 1; rep from * twice more, join with ss to top of beg ch-3.

Round 3: Ss to and into next ch-1 sp, ch 3 (counts as first dc), [1 dc, ch 1, 2 dc] in sp at base of ch-3, ch 1, *[2 dc, ch 1, 2 dc] in next ch-1 sp, ch 1; rep from * 6 times more, join with ss to top of beg ch-3.

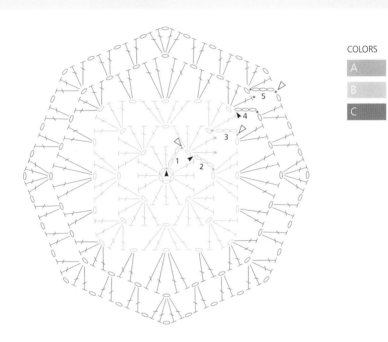

COLORS

A

B

C

Fasten off B. Join C to next ch-1 sp.

Round 4: Ch 3 (counts as first dc), [1 dc, ch 1, 2 dc] in sp at base of ch-3, ch 1, * 2 dc in next ch-1 sp, ch 1, [2 dc, ch 1, 2 dc] in next ch-1 sp, ch 1; rep from * 7 times more, join with ss to top of beg ch-3.

Round 5: Ss to and into next ch-1 sp, ch 3 (counts as first dc), [1 dc, ch 1, 2 dc] in sp at base of ch-3, ch 1, [2 dc in next ch-1 sp, ch 1] twice, *[2 dc, ch 1, 2 dc] in next ch-1 sp, ch 1, [2 dc in next ch-1 sp, ch 1] twice; rep from * 6 times more, join with ss to top of beg ch-3.

Fasten off.

70

Octagon Wheel

MEDIUM
- 4¾–6 in. (12–15 cm)
- Worsted yarn
- Size J (5.5 mm) hook

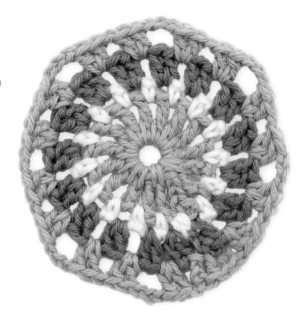

Foundation ring: Using A, ch 7, join with ss to form a ring.

Round 1: Ch 5 (counts as first tr and ch 1), [1 tr, ch 1] 15 times into ring, join with ss to fourth ch of beg ch-5.

Fasten off A. Join B to any ch-1 sp.

Round 2: Ch 1, 1 sc in sp at base of ch-1, ch 2, [1 sc in next ch-1 sp, ch 2] 15 times, join with ss to first sc.

Fasten off B. Join C to any ch-2 sp.

COLORS

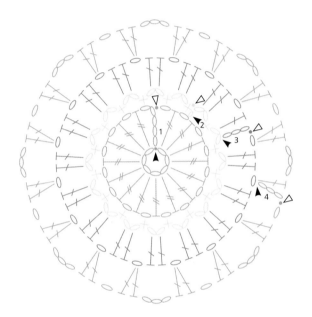

Round 3: Ch 3 (counts as first dc), 1 dc in sp at base of ch-3, ch 1, [2 dc in next ch-2 sp, ch 1] 15 times, join with ss to top of beg ch-3.

Fasten off C. Join A to any ch-1 sp.

Round 4: Ch 3 (counts as first dc), 1 dc in sp at base of ch-3, ch 3, 2 dc in next ch-1 sp, ch 1, [2 dc in next ch-1 sp, ch 3, 2 dc in next ch-1 sp, ch 1] 7 times, join with ss to top of beg ch-3.

Fasten off.

71

Octagon Frame

LARGE
- **6–7 in.**
  (15–18 cm)
- Light worsted
  yarn
- Size 7 (4.5 mm)
  hook

Foundation ring: Using A, make a magic ring.

Round 1: Ch 3 (counts as first dc), 7 dc into ring, join with ss to top of beg ch-3, turn.

Round 2: Ch 5 (counts as first dc and ch 2), [1 dc in next dc, ch 2] 7 times, join with ss to third ch of beg ch-5, turn.

Round 3: Ch 3 (counts as first dc), 2 dc in sp at base of ch-3, ch 3, [3 dc in next ch-2 sp, ch 3] 7 times, join with ss to top of beg ch-3, turn.

Round 4: Ch 3 (counts as first dc), 3 dc in sp at base of ch-3, ch 4, [4 dc in next ch-3 sp, ch 4] 7 times, join with ss to top of beg ch-3, turn.

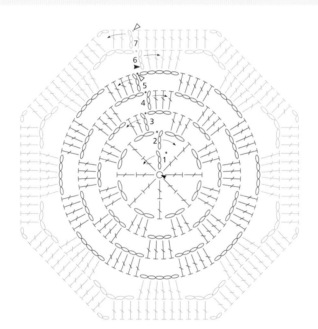

COLORS

A

B

Round 5: Ch 3 (counts as first dc), 4 dc in sp at base of ch-3, ch 5, [5 dc in next ch-4 sp, ch 5] 7 times, join with ss to top of beg ch-3, turn.

Fasten off A. Join B.

Round 6: Ch 3 (counts as first dc), 5 dc in sp at base of ch-3, ch 5, [6 dc in next ch-5 sp, ch 5] 7 times, join with ss to top of beg ch-3, turn.

Round 7: Ch 3 (counts as first dc), [2 dc, ch 2, 3 dc] in sp at base of ch-3, 1 dc in each of next 6 dc, [(3 dc, ch 2, 3 dc) in next ch-5 sp, 1 dc in each of next 6 dc] 7 times, join with ss to top of beg ch-3.

Fasten off.

Two-tone Bobble Octagon

LARGE
- 6–7 in. (15–18 cm)
- Worsted yarn
- Size J (5.5 mm) hook

Foundation ring: Using A, ch 4, join with ss to form a ring.

Round 1: Ch 5 (counts as first dc and ch 2), [1 dc into ring, ch 2] 7 times, join with ss to third ch of beg ch-5.

Round 2: Ch 3 (counts as first dc), 2 dc in st at base of ch-3, ch 2, [3 dc in next dc, ch 2] 7 times, join with ss to top of beg ch-3.

Round 3: Ch 3 (counts as first dc), 1 dc in st at base of ch-3, 1 dc in next dc, 2 dc in next dc, ch 2, [2 dc in next dc, 1 dc in next dc, 2 dc in next dc, ch 2) 7 times, join with ss to top of beg ch-3.

Fasten off A. Join B.

Round 4: Ch 5 (counts as first dc and ch 2), skip 1 dc, MB in next dc, ch 2, skip 1 dc, 1 dc in next dc, ch 2, [1 dc in next dc, ch 2, skip 1 dc, MB in next dc, ch 2, skip 1 dc, 1 dc in next dc, ch 2] 7 times, join with ss to third ch of beg ch-5. Fasten off B. Join A.

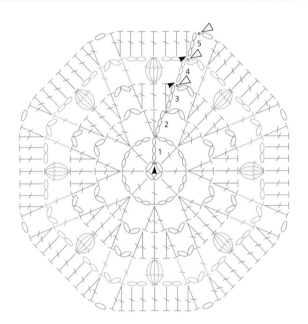

COLORS

A

B

Round 5: Ch 3 (counts as first dc), 1 dc in st at base of ch-3, 2 dc in next ch-2 sp, 1 dc in top of next bobble, 2 dc in next ch-2 sp, 2 dc in next dc, ch 1, [2 dc in next dc, 2 dc in next ch-2 sp, 1 dc in top of next bobble, 2 dc in next ch-2 sp, 2 dc in next dc, ch 1] 7 times, join with ss to top of beg ch-3.

Fasten off.

SPECIAL ABBREVIATION

MB (make bobble): [Yo, insert hook in st, yo, draw yarn through, yo, draw through 2 loops on hook] 5 times in same st, yo, draw through all 6 loops on hook.

73 Celtic Octagon

MEDIUM
- 4¾–6 in. (12–15 cm)
- Worsted yarn
- Size J (5.5 mm) hook

Foundation ring: Using A, ch 6, join with ss to form a ring.

Round 1: [Ch 4, 3 tr into ring, ch 4, ss into ring] 4 times.

Fasten off A. Join B.

Round 2: Ch 6 (counts as first dc and ch 3), skip (ch-4 sp, 3 tr, ch-4 sp), *[1 dc, ch 3, 1 dc] in next ss, ch 3, skip (ch-4 sp, 3 tr, ch-4 sp); rep from * twice more, 1 dc in next ss, ch 3, join with ss to third ch of beg ch-6.

Round 3: Ch 5, *3 tr in sp at base of ch-5, ch 4, 1 sc in next dc, ch 4; rep from * 6 times more, 3 tr in next ch-3 sp, ch 4, join with ss to first ch of beg ch-5.

Fasten off B. Join C.

Round 4: Ch 5, *skip (ch-4 sp, 3 tr, ch-4 sp), 1 sc in next sc, ch 4; rep from * 6 times more, skip (ch-4 sp, 3 tr, ch-4 sp), join with ss to first ch of beg ch-5.

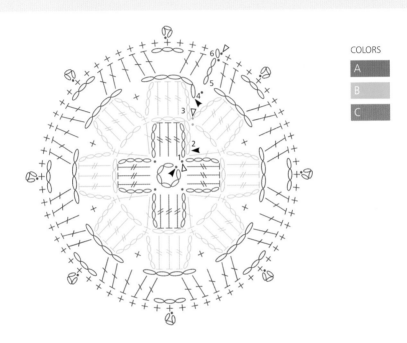

COLORS

A

B

C

Round 5: Ch 3 (counts as first dc), [2 dc, ch 3, 2 dc] in sp at base of ch-3, [1 dc in next sc, (2 dc, ch 3, 2 dc) in next ch-4 sp] 7 times, join with ss to top of beg ch-3.

Round 6: Ch 1, 1 sc in each of next 2 dc, *2 sc in next ch-3 sp, ch 3, ss in last sc made, 1 sc in same ch-3 sp, 1 sc in each of next 5 dc; rep from * 6 times more, 2 sc in next ch-3 sp, ch 3, ss in last sc made, 1 sc in same ch-3 sp, 1 sc in each of next 2 dc, join with ss to beg ch-1.

Fasten off.

Arrange petals of round 3 in front of round 4, and petals of round 1 in front of round 2.

74 Tri-color Bullseye

LARGE
- 6–7 in.
  (15–18 cm)
- Worsted yarn
- Size J (5.5 mm)
  hook

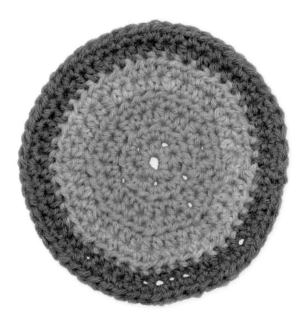

Foundation ring: Using A, ch 4, join with ss to form a ring.

Round 1: Ch 2, 8 hdc into ring, join with ss to top of beg ch-2, turn. (8 sts)

Round 2: Ch 2, 2 hdc in each hdc around, join with ss to top of beg ch-2, turn. (16 sts)

Round 3: Ch 2, [1 hdc in next hdc, 2 hdc in next hdc] 8 times, join with ss to top of beg ch-2, turn. (24 sts)

Round 4: Ch 2, [1 hdc in each of next 2 hdc, 2 hdc in next hdc] 8 times, join with ss to top of beg ch-2, turn. (32 sts)

Fasten off A. Join B.

Round 5: Ch 2, [1 hdc in each of next 3 hdc, 2 hdc in next hdc] 8 times, join with ss to top of beg ch-2, turn. (40 sts)

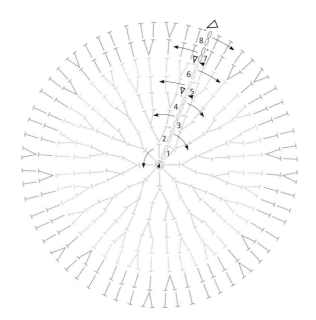

Round 6: Ch 2, [1 hdc in each of next 4 hdc, 2 hdc in next hdc] 8 times, join with ss to top of beg ch-2, turn. (48 sts)

Fasten off B. Join C.

Round 7: Ch 2, 1 hdc in each of next 3 hdc, 2 hdc in next hdc, [1 hdc in each of next 5 hdc, 2 hdc in next hdc] 7 times, 1 hdc in each of next 2 hdc, join with ss to top of beg ch-2, turn. (56 sts)

Round 8: Ch 2, 1 hdc in each of next 4 hdc, 2 hdc in next hdc, [1 hdc in each of next 6 hdc, 2 hdc in next hdc] 7 times, 1 hdc in each of next 2 hdc, join with ss to top of beg ch-2, turn. (64 sts)

Fasten off.

75 Picot Spiral

LARGE

- 6–7 in.
  (15–18 cm)
- Worsted yarn
- Size J (5.5 mm)
  hook

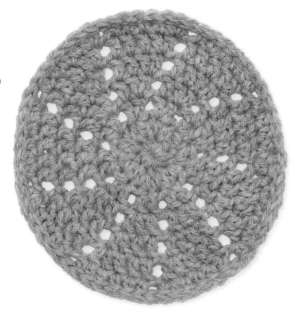

Foundation ring: Ch 4, join with ss to form a ring.

Round 1: Ch 1, 9 sc into ring, do not join.

Round 2: [2 hdc in next sc] 9 times.

Round 3: [2 dc in next hdc, ch 1, skip 1 hdc] 9 times.

Round 4: [2 dc in next dc, 1 dc in next dc, ch 1, skip ch-1 sp] 9 times.

Round 5: [2 dc in next dc, 1 dc in each of next 2 dc, ch 1, skip ch-1 sp] 9 times.

Round 6: [2 dc in next dc, 1 dc in each of next 3 dc, ch 1, skip ch-1 sp] 9 times.

COLOR

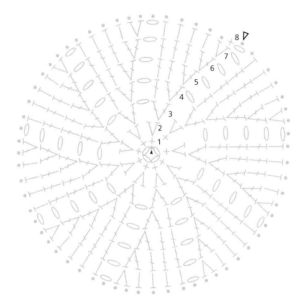

Round 7: [2 hdc in next dc, 1 hdc in each of next 4 dc, ch 1, skip ch-1 sp] 9 times.

Round 8: 1 sc in next hdc, ss in each hdc and ch-1 sp around.

Fasten off.

NOTE

Mark beginning of round with a detachable marker or safety pin and move the marker up as you work.

76 Tri-color Granny Circle

LARGE

- 6–7 in.
  (15–18 cm)
- Worsted yarn
- Size J (5.5 mm)
  hook

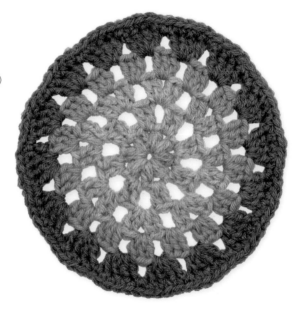

Foundation ring: Using A, ch 4, join with ss to form a ring.

Round 1: Ch 3, 1 hdc into ring (counts as first puff st), ch 1, [puff st into ring, ch 1] 7 times, join with ss to top of first puff st.

Round 2: Ss in next ch-1 sp, ch 3 (counts as first dc), 1 dc in sp at base of ch-3, ch 2, [2 dc in next ch-1 sp, ch 2] 7 times, join with ss to top of beg ch-3.

Round 3: Ss in next ch-2 sp, ch 3 (counts as first dc), [1 dc, ch 1, 2 dc] in sp at base of ch-3, ch 1, *[2 dc in next ch-2 sp, ch 1] twice; rep from * 6 times more, join with ss to top of beg ch-3.

Fasten off A. Join B to next ch-1 sp.

Round 4: Ch 3 (counts as first dc), 2 dc in sp at base of ch-3, ch 1, [3 dc in next ch-1 sp, ch 1] 15 times, join with ss to top of beg ch-3.

Fasten off B. Join C to next ch-1 sp.

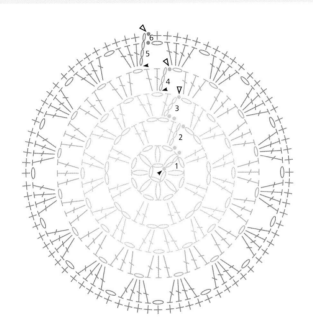

COLORS

A

B

C

Round 5: Ch 3 (counts as first dc), 3 dc in sp at base of ch-3, ch 1, [4 dc in next ch-1 sp, ch 1] 15 times, join with ss to top of beg ch-3.

Round 6: Ch 1 (counts as first sc), 1 sc in each dc and ch-1 sp around, join with ss to beg ch-1.

Fasten off.

SPECIAL ABBREVIATION

puff st: [Yo, insert hook into foundation ring, draw yarn through] twice, yo, draw through all 5 loops on hook.

Water Wheel

LARGE
- 6–7 in.
  (15–18 cm)
- Worsted yarn
- Size J (5.5 mm)
  hook

Foundation ring: Ch 4, join with ss to form a ring.

Round 1: Ch 3 (counts as first dc), 1 dc into ring, [ch 2, 2 dc into ring] 5 times, ch 2, join with ss to top of beg ch-3.

Round 2: Ch 3 (counts as first dc), 2 dc in st at base of ch-3, 1 dc in next dc, *ch 3, skip 2 ch, 3 dc in next dc, 1 dc in next dc; rep from * 4 times more, ch 3, skip 2 ch, join with ss to top of beg ch-3.

Round 3: Ch 3 (counts as first dc), 2 dc in st at base of ch-3, 1 dc in next dc, dc2tog over next 2 dc, *ch 4, skip 3 ch, 3 dc in next dc, 1 dc in next dc, dc2tog over next 2 dc; rep from * 4 times more, ch 4, skip 3 ch, join with ss to top of beg ch-3.

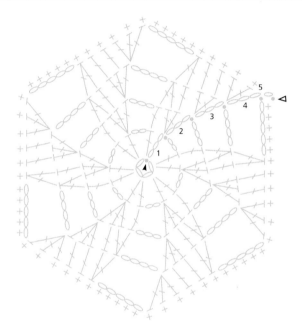

COLOR

Round 4: Ch 3 (counts as first dc), 2 dc in st at base of ch-3, 1 dc in each of next 2 dc, dc2tog over next 2 dc, *ch 5, skip 4 ch, 3 dc in next dc, 1 dc in each of next 2 dc, dc2tog over next 2 dc; rep from * 4 times more, ch 5, skip 4 ch, join with ss to top of beg ch-3.

Round 5: Ch 1 (counts as first sc), 1 sc in each dc and ch around, join with ss to beg ch-1.

Fasten off.

78 Color Swirl Circle

LARGE
- 6–7 in.
  (15–18 cm)
- Worsted yarn
- Size J (5.5 mm)
  hook

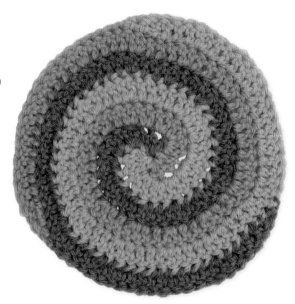

Foundation chain: Using A, ch 2.

Round 1: Working into second ch from hook, [1 sc, 1 hdc, 2 dc] in ch, remove hook from loop A, join B with sc in same ch, [1 hdc, 2 dc] in same ch, remove hook from loop B, join C with sc in same ch, [1 hdc, 2 dc] in same ch, remove hook from loop C, gently tighten chain into which sts have been worked. (4 sts in each color)

Round 2: Using A, *2 dc in each of next 4 sts, remove hook from loop A; rep from * with colors B and C. (8 sts in each color)

Round 3: Using A, *[2 dc in next st, 1 dc in next st] 4 times, remove hook from loop A; rep from * with colors B and C. (12 sts in each color)

Round 4: Using A, *[2 dc in next st, 1 dc in each of next 2 sts] 4 times, remove hook from loop A; rep from * with colors B and C. (16 sts in each color)

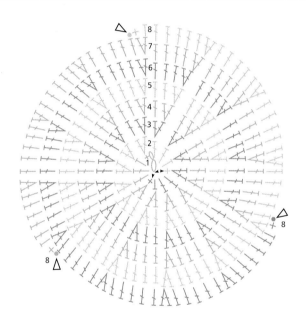

COLORS

A

B

C

Round 5: Using A, *[2 dc in next st, 1 dc in each of next 3 sts] 4 times, remove hook from loop A; rep from * with colors B and C. (20 sts in each color)

Round 6: Using A, *[2 dc in next st, 1 dc in each of next 4 sts] 4 times, remove hook from loop A; rep from * with colors B and C. (24 sts in each color)

Round 7: Using A, *[2 dc in next st, 1 dc in each of next 5 sts] 4 times, remove hook from loop A; rep from * with colors B and C. (28 sts in each color)

Round 8: Using A, *1 hdc in next st, 1 sc in next st, ss in next st, fasten off A; rep from * with B and C.

NOTE
Place working loops not in use onto a split-ring marker or safety pin.

79 Geometric Wheel

LARGE
- 6–7 in. (15–18 cm)
- Worsted yarn
- Size J (5.5 mm) hook

Foundation ring: Ch 10, join with ss to form a ring.

Round 1: Ch 3 (counts as first dc), 29 dc into ring, join with ss to top of beg ch-3. (30 dc)

Round 2: Ch 6 (counts as first dc and ch 3), skip 2 dc, [1 dc in next dc, ch 3, skip 2 dc] 9 times, join with ss to third ch of beg ch-6.

COLOR

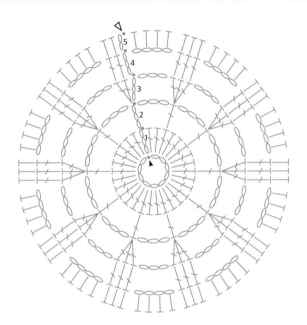

Round 3: Ch 3 (counts as first dc), 2 dc in st at base of ch-3, ch 3, [3 dc in next dc, ch 3] 9 times, join with ss to top of beg ch-3.

Round 4: Ch 3 (counts as first dc), 1 dc in each of next 2 dc, ch 4, [1 dc in each of next 3 dc, ch 4] 9 times, join with ss to top of beg ch-3.

Round 5: Ch 2 (counts as first hdc), 1 hdc in each dc and ch around, join with ss to top of beg ch-2.

Fasten off.

80 Tri-color Medallion

SMALL

- 3½–4¾ in. (9–12 cm)
- Worsted yarn
- Size J (5.5 mm) hook

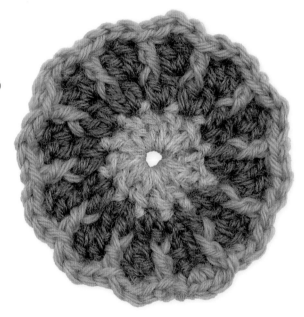

Foundation ring: Using A, ch 4, join with ss to form a ring.

Round 1: Ch 3 (counts as first dc), 11 dc into ring, join with ss to top of beg ch-3.

Fasten off A. Join B.

Round 2: Ch 3 (counts as first dc), 1 dc in st at base of ch-3, 2 dc in each st around, join with ss to top of beg ch-3.

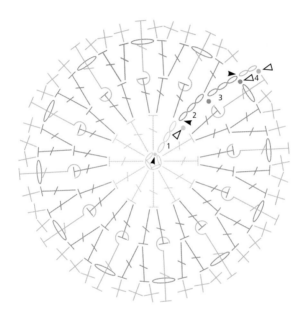

COLORS

A

B

C

Round 3: Ch 3 (counts as first dc), 1 dc in st at base of ch-3, ch 1, skip 1 st, *2 dc in next st, ch 1, skip 1 st; rep from * 10 times more, join with ss to top of beg ch-3.

Fasten off B. Join C.

Round 4: Ch 2 (counts as first sc), 2 sc in next dc, working in front of next ch-1 sp FPdc around skipped st of round 2, *1 sc in next dc, 2 sc in next dc, working in front of next ch-1 sp FPdc around skipped st of round 2; rep from * 10 times more, join with ss to top of beg ch-2.

Fasten off.

81

Popcorn Circle

MEDIUM
- 4¾–6 in. (12–15 cm)
- Worsted yarn
- Size J (5.5 mm) hook

Foundation ring: Using A, make a magic ring.

Round 1: Ch 3 (counts as first dc), 15 dc into ring, join with ss to top of beg ch-3.

Round 2: Beg popcorn, 2 dc in next dc, [popcorn in next dc, 2 dc in next dc] 7 times, join with ss to top of beg popcorn.

Round 3: Ch 3 (counts as first dc), 2 dc in top of popcorn at base of ch-3, 1 dc in next dc, [2 dc in next st or popcorn, 2 dc in next st or popcorn] 11 times, join with ss to top of beg ch-3.

Fasten off A. Join B.

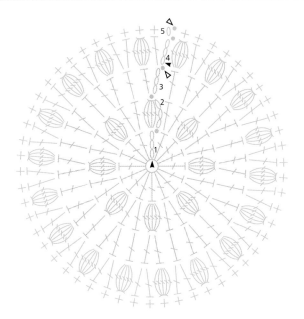

COLORS

A

B

Round 4: Ch 3 (counts as first dc), 1 dc in st at base of ch-3, popcorn in next dc, [2 dc in next dc, popcorn in next dc] 17 times, join with ss to top of beg ch-3.

Round 5: Ch 1 (counts as first sc), 1 sc in each st or popcorn around, join with ss to beg ch-1.

Fasten off.

SPECIAL ABBREVIATIONS

beg popcorn: Ch 3, 4 dc in st at base of ch-3, remove hook from working loop, insert hook in top of first dc of popcorn, catch working loop, yo, draw through loop and st.

popcorn: 5 dc in next st, remove hook from working loop, insert hook in top of first dc of popcorn, catch working loop, yo, draw through loop and st.

82 Post Stitch Spoke Wheel

LARGE

- 6–7 in. (15–18 cm)
- Worsted yarn
- Size J (5.5 mm) hook

Foundation ring: Ch 4, join with ss to form a ring.

Round 1: Ch 3 (counts as first dc), 11 dc into ring, join with ss to top of beg ch-3. (12 sts)

Round 2: Ch 3 (counts as first dc), FPdc around beg ch-3 of round 1, [1 dc in next dc, FPdc around dc at base of last dc worked] 11 times, join with ss to top of beg ch-3. (24 sts)

Round 3: Ch 3 (counts as first dc), 1 dc in next st, FPdc around FPdc at base of last dc worked, [1 dc in each of next 2 sts, FPdc around FPdc at base of last dc worked] 11 times, join with ss to top of beg ch-3. (36 sts)

Round 4: Ch 3 (counts as first dc), 1 dc in each of next 2 sts, FPdc around FPdc at base of last dc worked, [1 dc in each of next 3 sts, FPdc around FPdc at base of last dc worked] 11 times, join with ss to top of beg ch-3. (48 sts)

COLOR

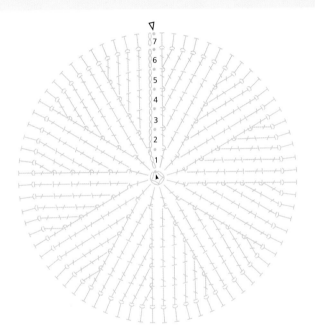

Round 5: Ch 3 (counts as first dc), 1 dc in each of next 3 sts, FPdc around FPdc at base of last dc worked, [1 dc in each of next 4 sts, FPdc around FPdc at base of last dc worked] 11 times, join with ss to top of beg ch-3. (60 sts)

Round 6: Ch 3 (counts as first dc), 1 dc in each of next 4 sts, FPdc around FPdc at base of last dc worked, [1 dc in each of next 5 sts, FPdc around FPdc at base of last dc worked] 11 times, join with ss to top of beg ch-3. (72 sts)

Round 7: Ch 2 (counts as first hdc), 1 hdc tbl in each st around, join with ss to top of beg ch-2. (72 sts)

Fasten off.

83 Flower Medallion

MEDIUM
- 4¾–6 in. (12–15 cm)
- Worsted yarn
- Size J (5.5 mm) hook

Foundation ring: Using A, ch 6, join with ss to form a ring.

Round 1: Ch 4 (counts as first tr), 2 tr into ring, [ch 1, 3 tr into ring] 5 times, ch 1, join with ss to top of beg ch-4, turn.

Fasten off A. Join B.

Round 2: Ss in next ch-1 sp, ch 7 (counts as 1 sc and ch 6), [1 sc in next ch-1 sp, ch 6] 5 times, join with ss to first ch of beg ch-7, do not turn.

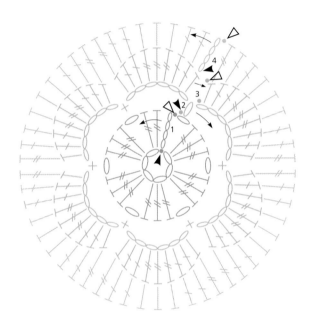

COLORS

A

B

C

Round 3: Ss in next ch-6 sp, [1 hdc, 2 dc, 3 tr, 2 dc, 1 hdc] in each ch-6 sp around, join with ss to first hdc, turn. (6 petals)

Fasten off. Join C to first hdc of any petal.

Round 4: Ch 4 (counts as first tr), *1 dc in each of next 2 dc, 1 hdc in each of next 3 tr, 1 dc in each of next 2 dc, 1 tr in each of next 2 hdc; rep from * 5 times more, omitting last tr of last rep, join with ss to top of beg ch-4.

Fasten off.

84

Bobble Border Wheel

LARGE

- 6–7 in. (15–18 cm)
- Worsted yarn
- Size J (5.5 mm) hook

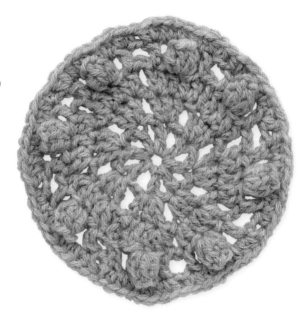

Foundation ring: Ch 4, join with ss to form a ring.

Round 1: Ch 5 (counts as first dc and ch 2), [1 dc into ring, ch 2] 7 times, join with ss to the third ch of beg ch-5.

Round 2: Ch 3 (counts as first dc), 2 dc in st at base of ch-3, ch 2, [3 dc in next dc, ch 2] 7 times, join with ss to top of beg ch-3.

Round 3: Ch 3 (counts as 1 dc), 1 dc in st at base of ch-3, 1 dc in next dc, 2 dc in next dc, ch 2, [2 dc in next dc, 1 dc in next dc, 2 dc in next dc, ch 2] 7 times, join with ss to top of beg ch-3.

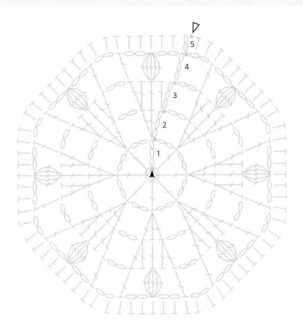

COLOR

Round 4: Ch 5 (counts as first dc and ch 2), skip 1 dc, MB in next dc, ch 2, skip 1 dc, 1 dc in next dc, ch 2, [1 dc in next dc, ch 2, skip 1 dc, MB in next dc, ch 2, skip 1 dc, 1 dc in next dc, ch 2] 7 times, join with ss to third ch of beg ch-5.

Round 5: Ch 2 (counts as first hdc), 1 hdc in each stitch and ch around, join with ss to top of beg ch-2.

Fasten off.

SPECIAL ABBREVIATION

MB (make bobble): Work 5 dc in next st, omitting final stage so that 1 loop of each remains on hook, yo, draw through all 6 loops on hook.

85

Spoke Wheel

EXTRA LARGE

- 7–8¼ in. (18–21 cm)
- Worsted yarn
- Size J (5.5 mm) hook

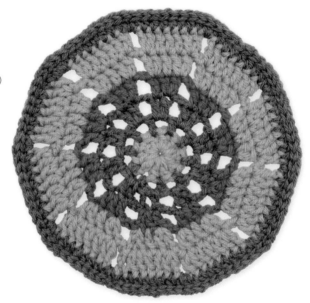

Foundation ring: Using A, ch 4, join with ss to form a ring.

Round 1: Ch 3 (counts as first dc), 9 dc into ring, join with ss to top of beg ch-3.

Fasten off A. Join B.

Round 2: Ch 4 (counts as first dc and ch 1), [1 dc in next dc, ch 1] 9 times, join with ss to third ch of beg ch-4.

Round 3: Ch 3, 1 dc in st at base of ch-3, ch 2, [2 dc in next dc, ch 2] 9 times, join with ss to top of beg ch-3.

Fasten off B. Join C.

Round 4: Ch 3, 1 dc in st at base of ch-3, 1 dc in next dc, ch 2, [2 dc in next dc, 1 dc in next dc, ch 2] 9 times, join with ss to top of beg ch-3.

Fasten off C. Join A.

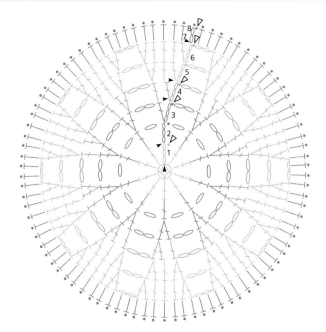

COLORS

A

B

C

Round 5: Ch 3, 1 dc in st at base of ch-3, 1 dc in next dc, 2 dc in next dc, ch 2, [2 dc in next dc, 1 dc in next dc, 2 dc in next dc, ch 2] 9 times, join with ss to top of beg ch-3.

Round 6: Ch 3 (counts as first dc), 1 dc in st at base of ch-3, 1 dc in each of next 3 dc, 2 dc next dc, ch 2, [2 dc in next dc, 1 dc in each of next 3 dc, 2 dc in next dc, ch 2] 9 times, join with ss to top of beg ch-3.

Fasten off A. Join B.

Round 7: Ch 2 (counts as first hdc), 1 hdc in each st and 2 hdc in each ch-2 sp around, join with ss to top of beg ch-2.

Round 8: Ss in each st around.

Fasten off.

86 Two-tone Lazy Wheel

LARGE

- 6–7 in.
  (15–18 cm)
- Worsted yarn
- Size J (5.5 mm)
  hook

Foundation ring: Using A, ch 17, join with ss to eighth ch.

Row 1: Working into ch-9 tail, 1 sc in second ch from hook, 1 hdc in next ch, 1 dc in next ch, 2 dc in next ch, 1 dc in next ch, 2 tr in next ch, 1 tr in next ch, 2 dtr in next ch, 1 dtr in next ch, do not turn.

Row 2: Working from left to right along row 1, reverse sc tfl in each st to end, ss into center ring, do not turn.

Remove hook from working loop. Join B to center ring.

Row 3: Working through back loop only of each st 2 rows below (behind reverse sc row), 1 sc in next st, 1 hdc in next st, 1 dc in next st, 2 dc in next st, 1 dc in next st, 2 tr in next st, 1 tr in next st, 2 dtr in next st, 1 dtr in next st.

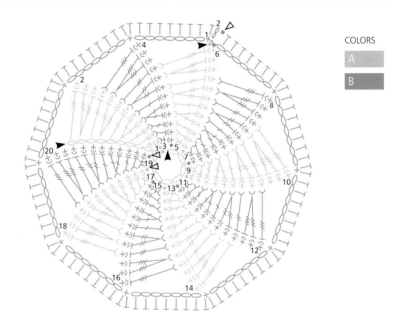

COLORS

A

B

Rep rows 2–3, alternating A and B, until 10 repeats have been completed.

Fasten off, leaving a 12 in. (30 cm) tail. Sew first and tenth repeats together through back loops of sts in row 19.

Join B to dtr at point of any repeat.

Round 1: Ch 1, 1 sc in dtr at base of ch-1, ch 7, [1 sc in next dtr, ch 7] 9 times, join with ss to first sc.

Round 2: Ch 2 (counts as first hdc), 1 hdc in st at base of ch-2, 7 hdc in next ch-7 sp, [2 hdc in next sc, 7 hdc in next ch-7 sp] 9 times, join with ss to top of beg ch-2.

Fasten off.

87

Bobble Swirl Motif

LARGE
- 6–7 in. (15–18 cm)
- Worsted yarn
- Size J (5.5 mm) hook

Foundation ring: Ch 6, join with ss to form a ring.

Round 1: 12 sc into ring, join with ss to first sc.

Round 2: Ch 4 (counts as first dc and ch 1), [1 dc in next sc, ch 1] 11 times, join with ss to third ch of beg ch-4.

Round 3: FPpuff st around beg ch-4 of round 2, *[ch 1, 1 dc, ch 1, 1 dc] in next ch-1 sp, FPpuff st around next dc; rep from * 10 times more, [ch 1, 1 dc, ch 1, 1 dc] in next ch-1 sp, join with ss to top of first FPpuff st.

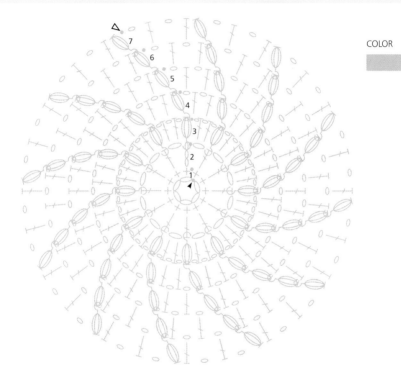

COLOR

Round 4: *FPpuff st around next FPpuff st, 1 dc between next 2 dc, ch 1, 1 dc between second dc and next FPpuff st, ch 1; rep from * 11 times more, join with ss to top of first FPpuff st.

Rep round 4, 3 times more.

Fasten off.

SPECIAL ABBREVIATION

FPpuff st (front post puff stitch): [Yo, insert hook from front to back to front around post of indicated stitch, draw yarn through] 4 times in same st, yo, draw through all 9 loops on hook.

88 Six-pointed Snowflake

MEDIUM
- 4¾–6 in. (12–15 cm)
- Worsted yarn
- Size J (5.5 mm) hook

Foundation ring: Ch 4, join with ss to form a ring.

Round 1: 6 sc into ring, join with ss to first sc.

Round 2: Ch 5 (counts as first dc and ch 2), 1 dc in first sc, *[1 dc, ch 2, 1 dc] in next sc; rep from * 4 times more, join with ss to third ch of beg ch-5.

Round 3: Ss in next ch-2 sp, ch 3 (counts as first dc), [1 dc, ch 3, 2 dc] in sp at base of ch-3, *[2 dc, ch 3, 2 dc] in next ch-2 sp; rep from * 4 times more, join with ss to top of beg ch-3.

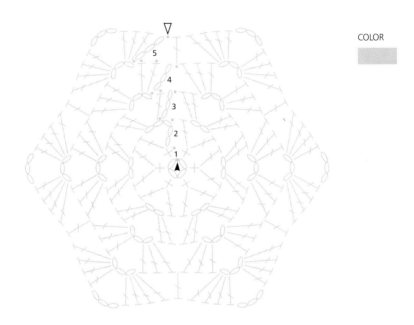

COLOR

Round 4: Ss to and into next ch-3 sp, ch 3 (counts as first dc), [2 dc, ch 3, 3 dc] in sp at base of ch-3, *[3 dc, ch 3, 3 dc] in next ch-3 sp; rep from * 4 times more, join with ss to top of beg ch-3.

Round 5: Ss to and into ch-3 sp, ch 3 (counts as first dc), [3 dc, ch 3, 4 dc] in sp at base of ch-3, *1 dc between 2 groups of dc, [4 dc, ch 3, 4 dc] in next ch-3 sp; rep from * 4 times more, 1 dc between 2 groups of dc, join with ss to top of beg ch-3.

Fasten off.

Two-tone Crystal Snowflake

MEDIUM
- 4¾–6 in. (12–15 cm)
- Worsted yarn
- Size J (5.5 mm) hook

Foundation ring: Using A, ch 4, join with ss to form a ring.

Round 1 (RS): Ch 3 (counts as first dc), 1 dc into ring, ch 1, [2 dc into ring, ch 1] 5 times, join with ss to top of beg ch-3.

Fasten off A. Join B to next ch-1 sp.

Round 2: Ch 3 (counts as first dc), [1 dc, ch 1, 2 dc] in sp at base of ch-3, *[2 dc, ch 1, 2 dc] in next ch-1 sp; rep from * 4 times more, join with ss to top of beg ch-3.

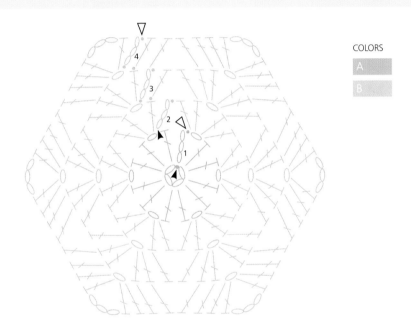

COLORS

A

B

Round 3: Ss to and into next ch-1 sp, ch 3 (counts as first dc), [1 dc, ch 1, 2 dc] in sp at base of ch-3, 1 dc in next dc, skip 2 dc, 1 dc in next dc, *[2 dc, ch 1, 2 dc) in next ch-1 sp, 1 dc in next dc, skip 2 dc, 1 dc in next dc; rep from * 4 times more, join with ss to top of beg ch-3.

Round 4: Ss to and into next ch-1 sp, ch 3 (counts as first dc), [1 dc, ch 3, 2 dc] in sp at base of ch-3, 1 dc in each of next 2 dc, skip 2 dc, 1 dc in each of next 2 dc, *[2 dc, ch 3, 2 dc] in next ch-1 sp, 1 dc in each of next 2 dc, skip 2 dc, 1 dc in each of next 2 dc; rep from * 4 times more, join with ss to top of beg ch-3.

Fasten off.

90 Pretty Snowflake

LARGE
- 6–7 in.
  (15–18 cm)
- Worsted yarn
- Size J (5.5 mm)
  hook

Foundation ring: Ch 9, join with ss to form a ring.

Round 1: Ch 8 (counts as first dc and ch 5), 3 dc into ring, [ch 5, 3 dc into ring] 4 times, ch 5, 2 dc into ring, join with ss to third ch of beg ch-8.

Round 2: Ss in each of next 2 ch, ch 7 (counts as first dc and ch 4), 4 dc in sp at base of ch-7, *ch 1, [4 dc, ch 4, 4 dc] in next ch-5 sp; rep from * 4 times more, ch 1, 3 dc in next ch-5 sp, join with ss to third ch of beg ch-7.

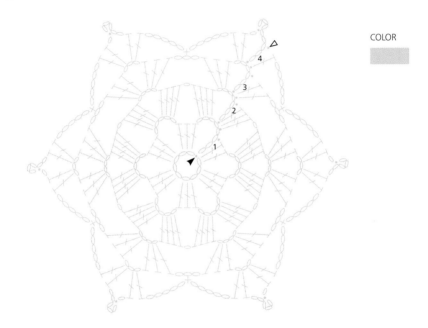

COLOR

Round 3: Ss in each of next 2 ch, ch 6 (counts as first dc and ch 3), 3 dc in sp at base of ch-6, *ch 3, [3 dc, ch 3, 3 dc] in next ch-4 sp; rep from * 4 times more, ch 3, 2 dc in next ch-3 sp, join with ss to third ch of beg ch-6.

Round 4: Ss in each of next 2 ch, ch 8, ss in fourth ch from hook, ch 1, 2 dc in sp at base of ch-8, ch 5, 1 sc in next ch-3 sp, *ch 5, [2 dc, ch 5, ss in fourth ch from hook, ch 1, 2 dc] in next ch-3 sp, ch 5, 1 sc in next ch-3 sp; rep from * 4 times more, ch 5, 1 dc in next ch-3 sp, join with ss to third ch of beg ch-8.

Fasten off.

91 Large Double Snowflake

EXTRA LARGE
- 7–8¼ in. (18–21 cm)
- Worsted yarn
- Size J (5.5 mm) hook

Foundation ring: Using A, ch 6, join with ss to form a ring.

Round 1: Ch 3 (count as first dc), 1 dc into ring, [ch 2, 2 dc into ring] 5 times, ch 2, join with ss to top of beg ch-3.

Round 2: Ch 3 (counts as first dc), 1 dc in st at base of ch-3, 2 dc in next dc, *[1 dc, 1 tr, picot, 1 dc] in next ch-2 sp, 2 dc in each of next 2 dc; rep from * 4 times more, [1 dc, 1 tr, picot, 1 dc] in next ch-2 sp, join with ss to top of beg ch-3.

Fasten off A. Join B with ss to top of last picot.

Round 3: *Ch 5, ss in picot sp at base of ch-5, ch 9, ss in top of next picot; rep from * 5 times more, join with ss to base of beg ch-5.

Round 4: *Ss in next ch-5 sp, ch 6, ss in sp at base of ch-6, 9 sc in next ch-9 sp; rep from * 5 times more, join with ss to beg ch-5 sp.

COLORS

A

B

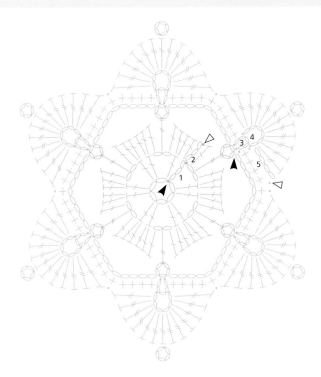

Round 5: Ch 4 (counts as first tr), 6 tr in next ch-6 sp, picot, 6 tr in same ch-6 sp, *skip 4 sc, ss in next sc, skip 4 sc, 7 tr in next ch-6 sp, picot, 6 tr in same ch-6 sp; rep from * 4 times more, skip 4 sc, ss in next sc, skip 4 sc, join with ss to top of beg ch-4.

Fasten off.

SPECIAL ABBREVIATION
Picot: Ch 5, ss in st at base of ch-5.

92 Double Crochet Star

MEDIUM
- 4¾–6 in.
  (12–15 cm)
- Worsted yarn
- Size J (5.5 mm)
  hook

Foundation ring: Ch 5, join with ss to form a ring.

Round 1: Beg 2-dc cl into ring, ch 3, [3-dc cl into ring, ch 3] 4 times, join with ss to top of beg 2-dc cl.

Round 2: Ss in next ch-3 sp, ch 3 (counts as first dc), [2 dc, ch 2, 3 dc] in sp at base of ch-3, *[3 dc, ch 2, 3 dc] in next ch-3 sp; rep from * 3 times more, join with ss to top of beg ch-3.

Round 3: Ss in next st, ch 3 (counts as first dc), 1 dc in next st, [3 dc, ch 2, 3 dc] in next ch-2 sp, 1 dc in each of next 2 sts, skip 2 sts, *1 dc in each of next 2 sts, [3 dc, ch 2, 3 dc] in next ch-2 sp, 1 dc in each of next 2 sts, skip 2 sts; rep from * 3 times more, join with ss to top of beg ch-3.

COLOR

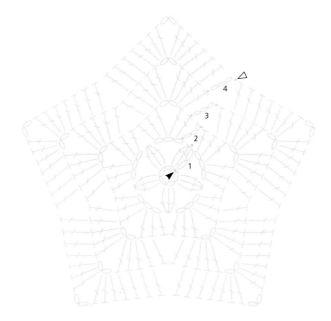

Round 4: Ss in next st, ch 3 (counts as first dc), 1 dc in each of next 3 sts, [3 dc, ch 2, 3 dc] in next ch-2 sp, 1 dc in each of next 4 sts, skip 2 sts, *1 dc in each of next 4 sts, [3 dc, ch 2, 3 dc] in next ch-2 sp, 1 dc in each of next 4 sts, skip 2 sts; rep from * 3 times more, join with ss to top of beg ch-3. Fasten off.

SPECIAL ABBREVIATIONS

beg 2-dc cl (beginning 2 double crochet cluster): Ch 2, [yo, insert hook into ring, yo, draw yarn through, yo, draw through 2 loops on hook] twice, yo, draw through all 3 loops on hook.

3-dc cl (3 double crochet cluster): [Yo, insert hook into ring, yo, draw yarn through, yo, draw through 2 loops on hook] 3 times, yo, draw through all 4 loops on hook.

93

Large Five-pointed Star

MEDIUM
- 4¾–6 in. (12–15 cm)
- Worsted yarn
- Size J (5.5 mm) hook

Foundation ring: Using A, ch 4, join with ss to form a ring.

Round 1: Ch 3 (counts as first dc), 14 dc into ring, join with ss to top of beg ch-3.

Round 2: Ch 3 (counts as first dc), [2 dc in next dc, 2 hdc in next dc, 2 dc in next dc] 5 times, ending 1 dc in st at base of beg ch-3, join with ss to top of beg ch-3.

First point

Row 3: Ch 3 (counts as first dc), 1 dc in next dc, dc2tog over next 2 hdc, 1 dc in each of next 2 dc, turn.

Row 4: Ch 2 (counts as first dc), dc4tog over next 3 sts and third ch of beg ch-3, ch 1. Fasten off.

COLORS

A

B

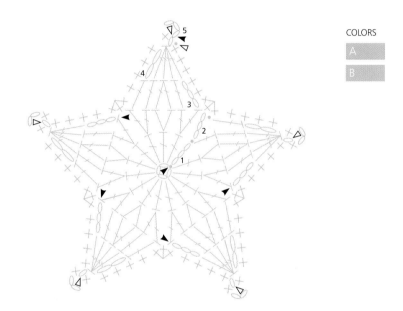

Remaining four points

Rejoin A to next unworked dc of round 2 and work second point as for first point.

Work three more points in the same way.

Join B to any point.

Round 5: Ch 3, 1 sc in st at base of ch-3, *4 sc down side edge of point, sc3tog at inner corner, 4 sc up side edge of next point, [1 sc, ch 2, 1 sc] at outer point; rep from * 4 times more, 4 sc down side edge of point, sc3tog at inner corner, 5 sc up side edge of next point, join with ss to first ch of beg ch-3.

Fasten off.

94
Lacy Five-pointed Star

MEDIUM
- 4¾–6 in. (12–15 cm)
- Worsted yarn
- Size J (5.5 mm) hook

Foundation ring: Ch 3, join with ss to form a ring.

Round 1: Ch 2 (counts as first hdc), 9 hdc into ring, join with ss to top of beg ch-2, turn.

Round 2: Ch 1, *[2 hdc, ch 2, 2 hdc] in next hdc, skip 1 hdc; rep from * 4 times more, join with ss to first hdc, turn.

Round 3: Ch 1, skip 1 hdc, *1 sc in next hdc, [2 sc, ch 2, 2 sc] in next ch-2 sp, 1 sc in next hdc, skip 2 hdc; rep from * to end of round, join with ss to first sc, turn.

COLOR

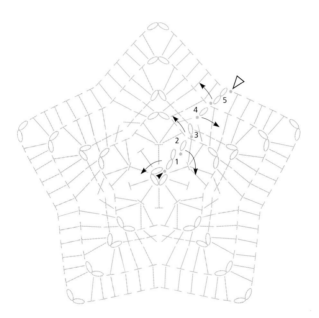

Round 4: Ch 1, skip first sc, *1 hdc in each of next 2 sc, [(2 hdc, ch 2, 2 hdc) in next ch-2 sp, 1 hdc in each of next 2 sc, skip 2 sc; rep from * to end of round, join with ss to first hdc, turn.

Round 5: Ch 2 (counts as first hdc), 1 hdc in each of next 4 hdc, *[2 hdc, ch 2, 2 hdc] in next ch-2 sp, 1 hdc in each of next 8 hdc; rep from * 3 times more, [2 hdc, ch 2, 2 hdc] in next ch-2 sp, 1 hdc in each of next 3 hdc, join with ss to first hdc.

Fasten off.

95

Six-pointed Star

SMALL
- 3½–4¾ in. (9–12 cm)
- Worsted yarn
- Size J (5.5 mm) hook

Foundation chain: Using A, ch 2.

Row 1: 1 sc in second ch from hook, turn. (1 st)

Row 2: Ch 1, 2 sc in sc, turn. (2 sts)

Row 3: Ch 1, 2 sc in first sc, 1 sc in next sc, turn. (3 sts)

Row 4: Ch 1, 2 sc in first sc, 1 sc in each of next 2 sc, turn. (4 sts)

Row 5: Ch 5, sc2tog over second and third chs from hook, 1 sc in each of next 2 ch, 1 sc in each of next 4 sc, 4 xsc, turn. (11 sts)

Row 6: Ch 1, sc2tog over first and second xsc, 1 sc in each st to end, turn. (10 sts)

Rep row 6, twice more. (8 sts)

Row 9: Ch 1, 2 sc in first sc, 1 sc in each sc to end, turn. (9 sts)

Rep row 9, 3 times more. (12 sts)

Row 13: Ch 1, ss in each of next 5 sc, ch 1, 1 sc in st at base of ch-1, 1 sc in each of next 3 sc, turn leaving last 4 sc unworked.

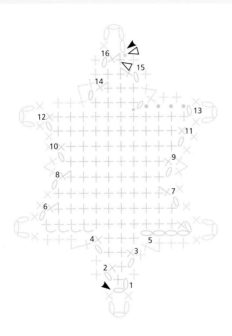

COLORS

A

B

Row 14: Ch 1, sc2tog over first and second sc, 1 sc in each of next 2 sc, turn.

Row 15: Ch 1, sc2tog over first and second sc, 1 sc in next sc, turn.

Row 16: Ch 1, sc2tog over remaining 2 sc, turn.

Fasten off A. Join B to any point.

Edging round: Ch 4, 1 sc in st at base of ch-4, *2 sc down side edge of point, sc2tog at inner corner, 2 sc up side edge of next point, [1 sc, ch 3, 1 sc] at outer point; rep from * 4 times more, 2 sc down side edge

of point, sc2tog at inner corner, 2 sc up side edge of next point, join with ss to first ch of beg ch-4. Fasten off.

SPECIAL ABBREVIATION

xsc (extended single crochet): Insert hook into base of last st, yo, draw yarn through, yo, draw through 1 loop on hook, yo, draw through both loops on hook.

96   Starburst Flower

LARGE

- 6–7 in.
  (15–18 cm)
- Worsted yarn
- Size J (5.5 mm)
  hook

Foundation ring: Using A, ch 6, join with ss to form a ring.

Round 1: Ch 3 (counts as first dc), 15 dc into ring, join with ss to top of beg ch-3. (16 sts)

Fasten off A. Join B.

Round 2: Ch 3 (counts as first dc), 2 dc in next dc, [1 dc in next dc, 2 dc in next dc] 7 times, join with ss to top of beg ch-3. (24 sts)

Fasten off B. Join C.

Round 3: Ch 3 (counts as first dc), 1 dc in st at base of ch-3, 2 dc in each of next 23 dc, join with ss to top of beg ch-3. (48 sts)

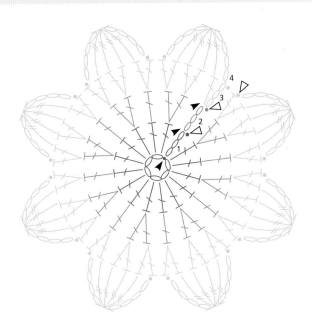

COLORS

A

B

C

Round 4: *Ch 4 (counts as first tr), tr4tog, ch 4, ss in next dc (petal made), ss in next dc; rep from * 6 times more, ch 4, tr4tog, ch 4, ss in next dc.

Fasten off.

SPECIAL ABBREVIATION

tr4tog (treble 4 stitches together): [(Yo) twice, insert hook in next st, draw yarn through, (yo, draw through 2 loops on hook) twice] 4 times, yo, draw through all 5 loops on hook.

97

Primrose

EXTRA LARGE
- 7–8¼ in.
  (18–21 cm)
- Worsted yarn
- Size J (5.5 mm)
  hook

Foundation ring: Using A, ch 6, join with ss to form a ring.

Round 1: Ch 6 (counts as first dc and ch 3), [1 dc into ring, ch 3] 6 times, join with ss to third ch of beg ch-6.

Round 2: [(1 sc, ch 4, 1 sc) in next ch-3 sp, (ss, ch 3, ss) in next dc] 6 times, [1 sc, ch 4, 1 sc] in next ch-3 sp, [ss, ch 3, ss] in third ch of beg ch-6.

Fasten off A. Join B to any ch-4 sp.

Round 3: Ch 3 (counts as first dc), [2 dc, ch 2, 3 dc] in sp at base of ch-3, *[3 dc, ch 2, 3 dc] in next ch-4 sp: rep from * 5 times more, join with ss to top of beg ch-3.

Round 4: Ss in next dc (center dc of 3-dc group), ch 3 (counts as first dc), 1 dc in next dc, *[2 dc, ch 2, 2 dc] in next ch-2 sp, 1 dc in each of next 2 dc, skip 2 dc, 1 dc in each of next 2 dc; rep from * 5 times more, [2 dc, ch 2, 2 dc] in next ch-2 sp, 1 dc in each of next 2 dc, skip last dc, join with ss to top of beg ch-3.

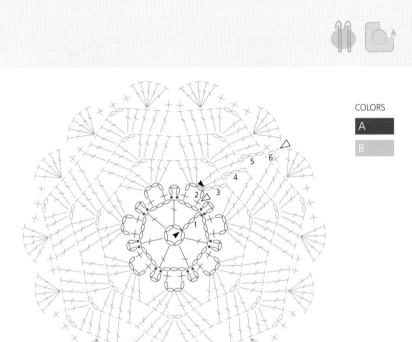

COLORS

A

B

Round 5: Ss in next dc, ch 3 (counts as first dc), 1 dc in each of next 2 dc, *[2 dc, ch 2, 2 dc] in next ch-2 sp, 1 dc in each of next 3 dc, skip 2 dc, 1 dc in each of next 3 dc; rep from * 5 times more, [2 dc, ch 2, 2 dc] in next ch-2 sp, 1 dc in each of next 3 dc, skip last dc, join with ss to top of beg ch-3.

Round 6: Ch 1, 1 sc in st at base of ch-1, *skip 1 dc, 5 dc in next dc (shell made), skip 1 dc, 1 sc in next dc, 1 sc in next ch-2 sp, 1 sc in next dc, skip 1 dc, 5 dc in next dc, skip 1 dc, 1 sc in each of next 2 dc; rep from * 5 times more, skip 1 dc, 5 dc in next dc, skip 1 dc, 1 sc in next dc, 1 sc in next ch-2 sp, 1 sc in next dc, skip 1 dc, 5 dc in next dc, skip 1 dc, 1 sc in next dc, join with ss to first sc.

Fasten off.

98 Sunflower

MEDIUM
- 4¾–6 in. (12–15 cm)
- Worsted yarn
- Size J (5.5 mm) hook

Foundation ring: Using A, ch 5, join with ss to form a ring.

Round 1: Ch 3 (counts as first dc), 15 dc into ring, join with ss to top of beg ch-3.

Fasten off A. Join B.

Round 2: Ch 1, 2 sc in st-sp between ch-3 and next dc, [2 sc in st-sp before next dc] 14 times, 2 sc in st-sp before ch-3, join with ss to beg ch-1.

Fasten off B. Join C.

Round 3: Ch 5 (counts as first dtr), skip first sc, dtr4tog tbl over next 4 sc, [ch 9, dtr5tog tbl over last st and next 4 sts] 7 times, ch 9, join with ss to top of beg dtr4tog.

Round 4: Ch 1, 9 sc in next ch-9 sp, [skip dtr5tog, 9 sc in next ch-9 sp] 7 times, join with ss to beg ch-1.

Fasten off.

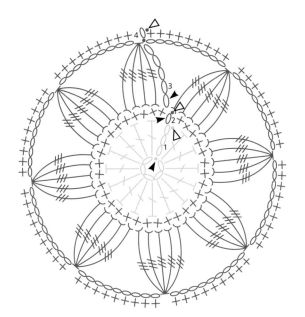

SPECIAL ABBREVIATIONS

dtr4tog tbl (double treble 4 stitches together through back loops): Working tbl of sts, *[yo] 3 times, insert hook in next st, yo, draw yarn through, [yo, draw through 2 loops on hook] 3 times; rep from * 3 times more, yo, draw through all 5 loops on hook.

dtr5tog tbl (double treble 5 stitches together through back loops): Working tbl of sts, [yo] 3 times, insert hook in same st as last st of previous cluster, yo, draw yarn through, [yo, draw through 2 loops on hook] 3 times, *[yo] 3 times, insert hook in next st, yo, draw yarn through, [yo, draw through 2 loops on hook] 3 times; rep from * 3 times more, yo, draw through all 6 loops on hook.

99 Two-tone Anemone

MEDIUM
- 4¾–6 in. (12–15 cm)
- Worsted yarn
- Size J (5.5 mm) hook

Foundation ring: Using A, ch 6, join with ss to form a ring.

Round 1: Ch 1, 24 sc into ring, join with ss to first sc.

Round 2: Ch 5 (counts as first dc and ch 2), 1 dc in next sc, [ch 1, skip 1 sc, 1 dc in next sc, ch 2, 1 dc in next sc] 7 times, ch 1, skip 1 sc, join with ss to third ch of beg ch-5.

Fasten off A. Join B to next ch-2 sp.

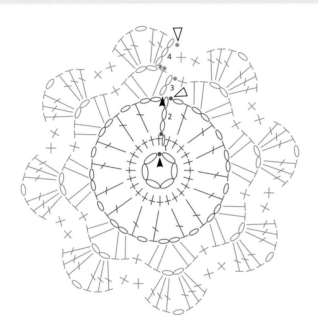

Round 3: Ch 2 (counts as first hdc), [1 hdc, ch 2, 2 hdc] in sp at base of ch-2, 1 sc in next ch-1 sp, *[2 hdc, ch 2, 2 hdc] in next ch-2 sp, 1 sc in next ch-1 sp; rep from * 6 times more, join with ss to top of beg ch-2.

Round 4: Ss to and into next ch-2 sp, ch 3 (counts as first dc), [2 dc, ch 1, 3 dc] in sp at base of ch-3, 1 sc in st-sp before next sc, 1 sc in st-sp after next sc, *[3 dc, ch 1, 3 dc] in next ch-2 sp, 1 sc in st-sp before next sc, 1 sc in st-sp after next sc; rep from * 6 times more, join with ss to top of beg ch-3.

Fasten off.

Dogwood

MEDIUM
- 4¾–6 in. (12–15 cm)
- Worsted yarn
- Size J (5.5 mm) hook

Foundation ring: Make a magic ring.

Round 1: Ch 1, 7 sc into ring, join with ss to beg ch-1.

Round 2: Ch 5, [skip 1 sc, 1 sc in next sc, ch 4] 3 times, join with ss to first ch of beg ch-5.

Round 3: Ss in next ch, ch 3 (counts as first dc), 6 dc in sp at base of ch-3, ch 2, skip 1 sc, [7 dc in next ch-4 sp, ch 2, skip 1 sc] 3 times, join with ss to top of beg ch-3.

Round 4: Ch 1, 1 sc in st at base of ch-1, [1 sc in each of next 2 dc, 2 sc in next dc] twice, skip 2 ch, *2 sc in next dc, [1 sc in each of next 2 dc, 2 sc in next dc] twice, skip 2 ch; rep from * twice more, join with ss to beg ch-1.

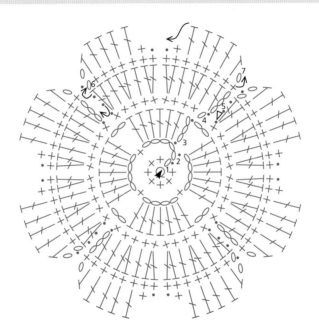

COLOR

Complete the first petal in rows as follows.

Row 5: Ch 3 (counts as first dc), 1 dc in st at base of ch-3, [1 dc in next sc, 2 dc in next sc] twice, 2 dc in next sc, [1 dc in next sc, 2 dc in next sc] twice, turn. (16 sts)

Row 6: Ch 1, skip first dc, 1 sc in each of 14 dc, 1 sc in top of beg ch-3, turn.

Row 7: Ch 1, skip first sc, 1 hdc in next sc, 1 dc in each of next 4 sc, 1 sc in next sc, ss in each of next 2 sc, 1 sc in next sc, 1 dc in each of next 4 sc, 1 hdc in last sc, ch 1, ss in beg ch-1 of row 6, 2 ss in side edge of dc below, 1 ss in side edge of sc below dc, 1 ss in next sc of round 4.

Rep rows 5–7, 3 times more, to complete each remaining petal.

Fasten off.

Techniques

Choosing Yarn

The blocks in this book are worked in light worsted- or worsted-weight yarn, but they can all be made with whatever yarn will work best for your project.

Questions to consider

As well as color, the fiber composition and the drape potential of a yarn are vital to the success of a project. Consider carefully the characteristics you require of the finished crocheted fabric.

- Would it be better if the fabric had some elasticity or not?
- Would a fabric with a good drape be better or one with a firm gauge and no drape?

Fit for purpose

If your proposed project is an afghan, then perhaps a soft, cozy fabric with good drape would be most suitable. Some people consider pure wool yarns preferable when crocheting an afghan or large project because wool is lighter than cotton and improves the drape of the crochet fabric; but there are times when synthetic yarns are better—particularly for baby items that may require frequent washing. For a bag, a firm, resilient fabric would be ideal, and for a pillow, well, the choice is up to you.

Test it out

Select a range of single balls or hanks of yarn and work a few sample blocks. With experience you will be able to gauge how a yarn may perform, but there are always surprises. Remember that the hook size and the block being worked will influence the final result—so experiment with yarns, hook sizes, and block patterns with more or less texture or loft.

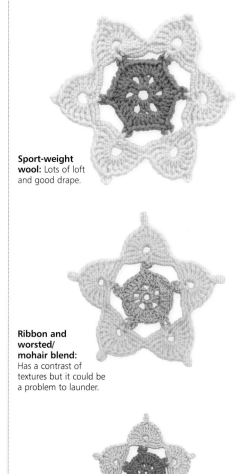

Sport-weight wool: Lots of loft and good drape.

Ribbon and worsted/ mohair blend: Has a contrast of textures but it could be a problem to launder.

Cotton: Holds the shape of the block well and has good stitch definition.

Getting Started

All of the blocks begin with a foundation chain (when working in rows) or a foundation ring or magic ring (when working in rounds). See page 212 for a reminder of how to work particular crochet stitches.

Slip knot
Wrap yarn into a loop, insert hook into loop, catch yarn with hook, and pull it through. Tighten loop on hook to form slip knot; this secures the yarn to the hook.

Foundation chain
Make the number of chain stitches specified in the pattern. Each V-shaped loop on the front is one chain stitch. The loop on the hook (the working loop) is not counted as a stitch. The first row of crochet stitches are worked into these chain stitches.

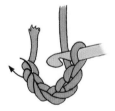

Foundation ring
Make a short length of foundation chain as specified in the pattern. Join the chains into a ring by working a slip stitch into the first chain. The first round of crochet stitches are worked into the center of the ring, not into the chain stitches.

Magic ring
Use this alternative to a foundation ring for working in the round when you want to avoid a hole in the center of your work. Wrap the yarn into a ring, insert the hook, and draw a loop through. Work the first round of crochet stitches into this ring, then pull the yarn tail tightly to close the ring.

Turning and starting chains

Extra chains are worked at the beginning of a row (turning chains) or round (starting chains) to bring the hook up to the correct height for the stitch you will be working next. Usually these chains count as the first stitch of the row or round, except for single crochet where the turning chain is ignored. Some blocks vary from the standard number of chains, and some count the turning chain as the first single crochet stitch. The pattern will always tell you when this is the case. A chain may also be longer than the number required for the stitch, and in that case counts as one stitch plus a number of chains. Again, the pattern will always explain this.

At the end of the row, the final stitch is usually worked into the turning chain of the previous row, either into the top chain of the turning chain or into another specified stitch of the chain. At the end of a round, the final stitch is usually joined to the starting chain with a slip stitch.

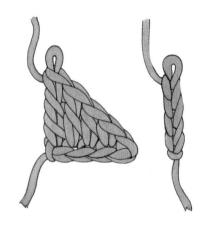

STANDARD NUMBER OF TURNING CHAINS
Single crochet (sc): 1 turning chain
Half double crochet (hdc): 2 turning chains
Double crochet (dc): 3 turning chains
Treble crochet (tr): 4 turning chains
Double treble crochet (dtr): 5 turning chains

Finishing the last round

For a neater finish, don't use a slip stitch to join the last stitch of the final round to the first stitch of the round. Instead, fasten off the yarn after the last stitch, thread a tapestry needle, and pass it under the top loops of the first stitch of the round and back through the center of the last stitch.

TIPS FOR NEAT EDGES WHEN WORKING IN ROWS
• Turn your work and take the working yarn around the outside to its new position and not over the top between the hook and the crochet edge.
• If you work the last stitch into the top of the turning chain and the edge bulges, pull out the last stitch and work it tightly into the chain below the top chain, to take in the slack.
• Rather than working into the top loops, work around the stem of the stitch, inserting the hook from back to front, around the post, and to the back again.
• If your chain stitches are tight, work an extra turning chain to stop the edges of the block from becoming too tight. If your chains are loose, work one less turning chain than specified.

Stitch Reminder

Here is a concise guide to the basic crochet stitches used to make the blocks.

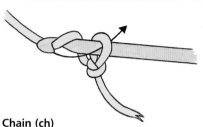

Chain (ch)
Wrap yarn over hook and draw it through loop on hook to form a new loop on hook.

Slip stitch (ss)
Insert hook into next stitch, wrap yarn over hook, and draw through stitch and loop on hook.

Single crochet (sc)
Insert hook into next stitch, yarn over hook, and draw through stitch (2 loops on hook). Yarn over hook and draw through both loops.

Extended single crochet (xsc)
Insert hook into next stitch, yarn over hook, and draw through stitch (2 loops on hook). Yarn over hook and draw through first loop (2 loops on hook). Yarn over hook and draw through both loops.

Half double crochet (hdc)
Yarn over hook, insert hook into next stitch, yarn over hook, and draw through stitch (3 loops on hook). Yarn over hook and draw through all three loops.

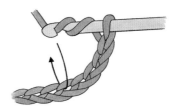

Double crochet (dc)
Yarn over hook, insert hook into next stitch, yarn over hook, and draw through stitch (3 loops on hook). *Yarn over hook and draw through two loops; repeat from * once more.

Treble crochet (tr)
Yarn over hook twice, insert hook into next stitch, yarn over hook, and draw through stitch (4 loops on hook). *Yarn over hook and draw through two loops; repeat from * twice more.

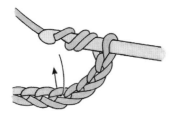

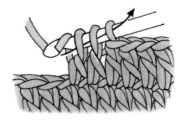

Double treble crochet (dtr)
Yarn over hook three times, insert hook into next stitch, yarn over hook, and draw through stitch (5 loops on hook). *Yarn over hook and draw yarn through two loops; repeat from * three times more.

Decrease (e.g. sc2tog, dc3tog)
Work specified number of stitches, omitting final stage of each stitch so that last loop of each stitch remains on hook. Wrap yarn over hook and draw through all loops on hook.

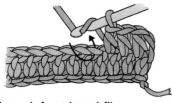

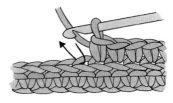

Through front loop (tfl)
Rather than inserting hook under both top loops to work the next stitch, insert it only under the front loop.

Through back loop (tbl)
Rather than inserting hook under both top loops to work the next stitch, insert it only under the back loop.

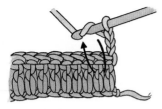

Front post (FP)
Work around the stem of the stitch, inserting hook from front to back, around the post, and to front again.

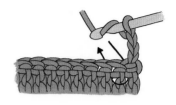

Back post (BP)
Work around the stem of the stitch, inserting hook from back to front, around the post, and to back again.

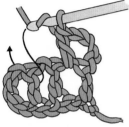

Chain space (ch sp)
Insert hook into space below chains. Here, a treble crochet stitch is being worked into a chain-1 space.

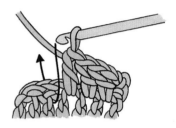

Stitch space (st-sp)
Insert hook between stitches of the previous row, instead of into top of stitch.

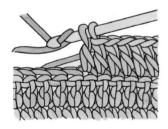

Joining yarn on a row
Work last stitch with old yarn, omitting final stage. Wrap new yarn over hook and draw through all loops on hook. The new yarn will form the top loops of the next stitch in the new color.

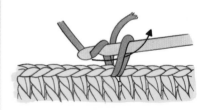

Joining yarn on a round
Method 1: Work joining slip stitch at end of round using new color. Method 2 (above): Insert hook where required, draw up a loop of new color leaving a 4 in. (10 cm) tail, and work specified number of starting chains. Continue with new yarn.

Cluster (cl)
Work specified number of stitches in places indicated in pattern, omitting final stage of each stitch so that last loop of each stitch remains on hook. Wrap yarn over hook and draw through all loops on hook.

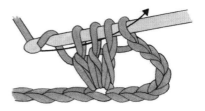

Bobble
Work specified number of stitches into same place, omitting final stage of each stitch so that last loop of each stitch remains on hook. Wrap yarn over hook and draw through all loops on hook.

Popcorn
Work specified number of stitches into same place. Take hook out of working loop and insert it under both top loops of first stitch of popcorn. Pick up working loop with hook and draw it through to fold the group of stitches and close the popcorn at the top.

Puff stitch
Work specified number of half double crochet stitches into same place, omitting final stage of each stitch so that two loops of each one remain on hook. Wrap yarn over hook and draw through all loops on hook.

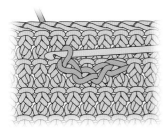

Surface crochet
Hold working yarn at back of finished block, insert hook from front to back through fabric in a space between two stitches, and pull through a loop. Insert hook between next two stitches and pull another loop through fabric and first loop on hook (like working a chain or slip stitch). Work around the posts of stitches, through gaps between stitches, or as specified in pattern.

Fitting Blocks Together

Some block shapes fit together easily to make a continuous surface with no gaps. Other types of blocks will not interlock exactly; the spaces between them can be left empty for a lighter, more lacy effect. Alternatively, the spaces between blocks can be filled with small connector pieces.

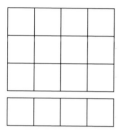

Squares
Join squares into strips, then join the strips to make the size and shape you want.

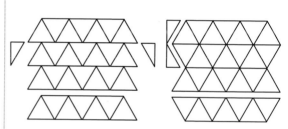

Triangles
Join triangles into strips, alternating the direction as required, then join the strips. Add half-triangles to the side edges if desired.

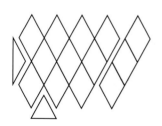

Diamonds
Assemble into diagonal strips, then join the strips. If you wish, work half-diamonds (triangles) to fit the gaps on the side edges.

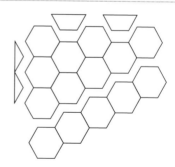

Hexagons
Join hexagons into diagonal strips, then join the strips to make the whole. Shallow triangles can fill the spaces on the side edges. The gaps on the top and bottom edges can be filled with half-hexagons.

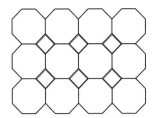

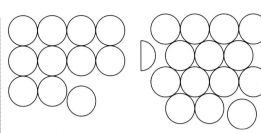

Octagons

Octagons can be joined with small square connectors set "on point" if required. Join one strip of octagons, matching opposite faces. Join the square connectors between them. Then add the octagons of the row below, one at a time. Repeat as required. Triangles may be used to fill the gaps around the edges.

Circles with spaces

Circles may be joined where they touch on four sides for an open, lacy effect. Join each circle in place in turn. For a firmer result, add connector pieces between the circles, as below. For smaller spaces without the use of connectors, join the circles in offset rows, and fill side edges with half-circles if desired.

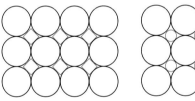

Circles with connectors

For a solid arrangement of circles, the gaps may be filled with small square connectors, stretched slightly to fit. Alternatively, using smaller circles as connectors leaves only small gaps between the shapes.

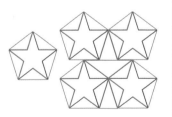

Stars and pentagons

Triangles added to a five-pointed star make a solid five-sided pentagon. Pentagons may be arranged in rows and the spaces filled with more triangles.

SNOWFLAKES AND FLOWERS

Shapes such as snowflakes have six points, and may therefore be treated as hexagons. Flowers may be treated as circles.

Planning Your Design

Make a visual plan of your design in order to check the final size and appearance, and to count how many blocks of each type and/or color you will need.

Planning stages

1 Measure your sample block(s), and decide on the finished size required. How many blocks will be required in each direction?

2 Draw each block to about 1 x 1 in. (2.5 x 2.5 cm), or as appropriate (don't draw too small). Large sheets of graph paper are helpful when drawing shapes such as squares, diamonds, and triangles. Other shapes are trickier to draw—if you have access to a computer with appropriate software, you can draw one shape such as a circle, then copy and paste it to make the arrangement you need. Otherwise, draw the shape of your sample block onto thin cardstock, then cut out the outline to make a template. Draw around the template, fitting the outlines closely together.

3 Roughly color in the plan to indicate the patterns and colors of your chosen blocks.

4 At the side of the plan, write a list of each block and colorway, and count how many blocks of each design will be needed.

5 Calculate the amount of yarn required of each color (see opposite).

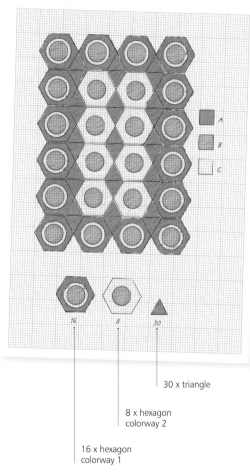

30 x triangle

8 x hexagon colorway 2

16 x hexagon colorway 1

Sketch for a hexagon blanket design

Gauge

Gauge refers to the number of stitches and rows to a given width and length of crochet fabric. It's important to crochet a test block before you start your project to establish what your gauge is.

If you want to match the size of the blocks shown in this book, work a sample block using the same yarn weight and hook size, and then block (see page 220) and measure your sample. As a rule, if your block is smaller than required, work another sample using a hook one size larger. If your block is larger, make another using a hook one size smaller.

Gauge can be affected by the color and fiber composition of the yarn and the size and brand of the crochet hook, so you may need to make several sample blocks using different hooks until you match the block size required.

When designing your own project, you need to establish the gauge that you want for the project. Work a sample block using your chosen yarn and the hook size that is recommended for that particular yarn, and then block the motif. If your block is smaller than required, make another sample using a hook one size larger. If your block fabric feels tight and hard, make another sample using a hook one size larger. If your block fabric feels loose and floppy, make another using a hook one size smaller. Continue to work sample blocks until you are happy with the size and feel of your crochet fabric.

A WORD OF CAUTION

Your gauge may vary depending on the stitch that dominates the block. For instance, you may need a larger hook for a block of single crochet, a slightly smaller hook for double crochet, and an even smaller hook for filet designs.

Calculating yarn amounts

The most reliable way to calculate how much yarn you need to buy for a specific project is to buy a ball of each yarn you are going to use for the project and then make some sample blocks.

The amount of yarn per ball or skein can vary considerably between colors of the same yarn because of the different dyes that have been used, so it's a good idea to make the samples using the actual colors you intend to use.

1 Using the yarn and a suitable size of hook, work three samples of each block you intend to use, making sure that you allow at least 3 in. (8 cm) of spare yarn at every color change. This will compensate for the extra yarn you will need for weaving in the ends.

2 Unravel the three blocks and carefully measure the amount of yarn used for each color in each block.

3 Take the average yardage and multiply it by the number of blocks you intend to make. Don't forget to add extra yarn to your calculations for joining the blocks together and for working any edgings.

4 Compare this yardage figure to the yardage of a whole ball (this information is usually printed on the ball band) and use this to calculate the number of balls to buy. If in doubt, always buy extra yarn.

Blocking and Joining

Always block your crochet before joining pieces together. This involves pinning blocks out to the correct size and then either steaming them with an iron or moistening them with cold water and allowing them to dry. Blocks can be joined by sewing or crocheting them together. Use the same yarn for joining as you used for working the blocks or a matching stronger yarn.

Blocking guidelines

Always be guided by the information given on the ball band of your yarn and, when in doubt, choose the cold water blocking method below.

1 Make a blocking board by securing one or two layers of quilter's batting, covered with a sheet of cotton fabric, over a 24 x 36 in. (60 x 90 cm) piece of flat board. Checked fabric is ideal because you can use the regular grid of checks to help with alignment of edges and points.

2 Pin out several blocks at the same time, using plenty of short metal pins. Gently ease the block into shape before inserting each pin.

3 To block woolen yarns with warm steam, hold a steam iron set at the correct temperature for the yarn about ¾ in. (2 cm) above the surface of the block and allow the steam to penetrate for several seconds.

4 Lay the board flat and allow the blocks to dry completely before removing the pins.

5 To block acrylic and wool/acrylic blend yarns, pin out the pieces as above, then use a spray bottle to mist the crochet with cold water until it is moist, but not saturated.

6 Gently pat the fabric to help the moisture penetrate more easily. Lay the board flat and allow the blocks to dry completely before removing the pins.

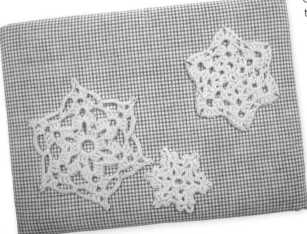

Blocking motifs with the right side up allows you to adjust the picots, bobbles, and other textured stitches so that they look their best.

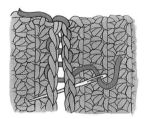

Woven seam

Lay the blocks with the edges touching and wrong sides facing upward. Using a tapestry needle, weave back and forth around the centers of the stitches, without pulling the stitches too tightly.

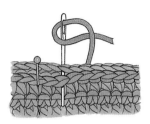

Backstitch seam

Hold the blocks to be joined with right sides together, pinning if necessary. Using a tapestry needle, work a line of backstitches along the edge.

Overcast seam

Using a tapestry needle, insert the needle into the back loops of corresponding stitches. For extra strength, work two stitches into the end loops.

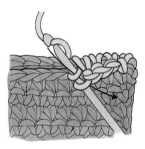

Single crochet seam

Work as for the slip stitch seam below, but work a row of single crochet stitch from the right or wrong side, depending on your preference.

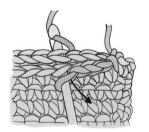

Slip stitch seam

Joining blocks with wrong sides together gives a firm seam with an attractive ridge on the right side. If you prefer the ridge not to be visible, join the blocks with right sides together so the ridge is on the wrong side. Work a row of slip stitch through both top loops of each block. When working this method along the side edges of blocks worked in rows, work enough evenly spaced stitches so that the seam is not too tight.

Reading Patterns and Charts

Block patterns are worked using a combination of stitches. In order to save space as well as make them easier to follow, abbreviations are used. Charts are visual representations of the written pattern and, once mastered, are quicker and easier to follow. All charts show the right side of the block.

Stitch symbol charts (all blocks)

All of the blocks in this book are accompanied by a stitch symbol chart. These show each type of stitch used in the block and where it is worked in relation to the other stitches. The stitches are colored to match the yarn colors used. A solid arrowhead indicates where a new yarn is joined; an outline arrowhead indicates where a yarn is fastened off.

Filet charts (blocks 1–12)

Filet patterns are very long when written out in full, making them appear far more complicated than they really are, so they are always worked from a chart. Filet designs are simply a sequence of "open mesh" spaces and "solid mesh" blocks. Each square on the chart represents two stitches, forming an open space or a solid block. Work the foundation chain as instructed in the written pattern, then follow the chart from row 1.

Colorwork charts (blocks 43–47)

Colorwork designs include a colored chart on a grid. It is easier to see the placement of colors on this type of chart. One square on the chart represents one stitch. Work the foundation chain as instructed in the written pattern, then follow the chart from row 1.

Charts in rows

All rows are numbered. Right-side rows start at the right, and are read from right to left. Wrong-side rows start at the left, and are read from left to right.

Charts in rounds

These begin at the center, and each round is usually read counterclockwise (the direction of working). When working blocks in the round, you will usually have the right side of the crochet facing you. Some blocks require you to turn the work, and this is indicated on the charts with an arrow pointing in the direction in which you should read the chart for that round. Each round is numbered near the beginning of the round.

Abbreviations and symbols

The list opposite includes the common crochet abbreviations and symbols. Any special abbreviations and instructions are explained with the relevant pattern.

ABBREVIATION AND SYMBOL VARIATIONS

Always read the list of abbreviations and symbols provided with the pattern you are using before starting a project. The abbreviations and symbols for the main stitches are standardized, but different pattern publishers and designers may use different ones for others, such as "flo" (front loop only) rather than "tfl" (through front loop).

Abbreviations

alt	alternate
beg	beginning
BP	back post
ch	chain
cl	cluster
cont	continue
dc	double crochet
dec	decrease
dtr	double treble
foll	follow(ing)
FP	front post
hdc	half double crochet
inc	increase
MB	make bobble
patt	pattern
rep	repeat
RS	right side
sc	single crochet
sp	space
ss	slip stitch
st(s)	stitch(es)
tbl	through back loop
tfl	through front loop
tog	together
tr	treble crochet
WS	wrong side
xsc	extended single crochet
yo	yarn over

Chart symbols

►	join yarn
▷	fasten off yarn
⌒	direction of working
O	magic ring
⊂	chain
•	slip stitch
+	single crochet
ⱦ	extended single crochet
T	half double crochet
ϯ	double crochet
ϯ	treble crochet
ϯ	double treble crochet
⋔	cluster (e.g. cluster of 3 dc)
⊕	bobble (e.g. bobble of 3 xsc)
⬯	puff stitch (e.g. puff of 5 hdc)
⬮	popcorn (e.g. popcorn of 4 dc)
⊼	through back loop (e.g. sc tbl)
⊥	through front loop (e.g. sc tfl)
ϳ	front post (e.g. FPdc)
ϳ	back post (e.g. BPtr)

Arrangement of symbols

JOINED AT TOP
A group of symbols joined at the top indicates that these stitches should be worked together at the top, as in cluster stitches, and for decreasing the number of stitches (e.g. sc2tog, dc3tog).

JOINED AT BASE
Symbols joined at the base should all be worked into the same stitch below.

JOINED AT TOP AND BASE
Sometimes a group of stitches are joined at both top and bottom, making a bobble, puff, or popcorn.

ON AN ANGLE
Symbols may be drawn at an angle, depending on the construction of the stitch pattern.

DISTORTED SYMBOLS
Some symbols may be lengthened, curved, or spiked, to indicate where the hook is inserted below.

Index

Credits

Quarto would like to thank the following for providing yarns used to make the blocks:

Lion Brand Yarns
www.lionbrand.com

Rowan Yarns
www.knitrowan.com

All photographs and illustrations are the copyright of Quarto Publishing plc. While every effort has been made to credit contributors, Quarto would like to apologize should there have been any omissions or errors—and would be pleased to make the appropriate correction for future editions of the book.